The

Transformation

Factor

Chief Apostle Dr. J. G. Rice

ISBN-13: 978-0692260807
ISBN-10: 0692260803

Publishers
Rice Ministries InterGlobal Publishing Company
5570 NW10th Terrace
Fort Lauderdale, Florida 33473

Mailing Address
P.O. Box 121436
Fort Lauderdale, Florida 33309

Publishers Contact Information
855-200-7729
www.kawebtv.com
www.chiefapostlerice.com

Publishing Company
Mygazine Publications
A division of Hills Management Group LLC
2901 Two Notch Road
Columbia, South Carolina 29204

803-200-1707
www.mygazinepubications.com

To Order Additional Copies of this book, contact
www.greaterhrvestworldwide.com
www.chiefapostlerice.com

Rice Ministries InterGlobal 1-855-200-7729
ghccstaff.mm@gmsail.com

This book was printed in the United States of America

DEDICATION

Our undying gratitude is always focused to God, his Son Christ Jesus, the Holy Spirit who teaches us all things and the powerful push of the 120 Prayer Partners of "Grace and Glory" who make these books possible for all to grow from.

To my blessings from above, for he is several in one, my faithful supportive husband **Arch Bishop James Rice.** I love you to life, for life! You give so much of me to the nations and the world, and you do it with a smile. Grace, Peace, Favor, and Abundance be declared to you 100 fold for all you push me to do!

To our Father, the awesome man of God, Deacon Calvin Moore, who prays for us and keeps us focused on the end results. To our Mother Bishop Doris Rice, who is filled with the power and glory of God, and reminds us, "you can do it". To our Spiritual Mother Martha T. Ruff, who has forced us to keep going unto the nations. All three which are currently in their eighties. I pray God will bless us with the strength, the mind, the health and the love they have for you at their age. They are still serving the Kingdom of God faithfully and gratefully. You three are truly my inspiration to get up early, work hard and stay up late to praise his Holy name.

To my Executive Assistant, Minister Stephanie JeanBaptiste, and my Adjutant, Deacon Shirley McInnis, whom become all things to be as we have a need... typists, travelers, coordinators, prayer warrior, schedule keepers, drivers, nurses and keeps me on my vitamins. I love you both.

To my friend and publisher, Elder Wilma Hills, always an unsung hero behind the greatness of so many great people and great works. You are a true Kingdom Ambassador and a gift to the body of Christ. You have inspired me to be a book writer and your level of excellence pushed me forward. Thank you for over 40 years of friendship .

To the "Clan" our Children, thanks for your sacrifice of letting us go and be who God has commanded us to be... we are so proud of you as you grow in the Lord.

To my "Church" children and others who are all so important to me, thanks again and here we go. You are the ones who REALLY make this happen. It's all about the Kingdom, it's in you. In fact it is you.

This book is dedicated especially to the Mentees and the writers in this book who dared to TRY to TRANSFORM and become different! Thanks for your stories, you have helped so many by just being honest.

If you love us, then this book is dedicated to you.

Dr J. G. Rice

Chief Apostle Dr J. G. Rice

CONTENTS

Introduction

THE TRANSFORMATION FACTOR

To transform in life, we must first pass the powerful "Test of Admissions." We must learn to overcome by *admitting that we need to change*. My slogan, "Admit it and Quit it. Then Replace it with something more powerful than you had before!" (This of course means positive things of replacement.) These positive atoms are needed to cause a stop gap on the desires in your life that were placed there by constant negative behaviors and reinforcements. In a moment of weakness or ingrained memories, these positive atoms can stop you from desiring to return to the negative behaviors of the past.

Beginning the Transformation Factor is the greatest and biggest step that you will ever take in life. To be "transformed" means that *YOU are willing to change*. It means that you realize that there is something deep down inside of you, that knows there's more to life than what is being expressed, provided, shown to or that you may have even been living in. When we make up in our minds to transform, we are saying we are going to become something different, smarter, better, stronger and more equipped for life than we have been before. A "factor" is a cause, or element that builds into one sum, to become another sum, purpose or thing.

So the **Transformation Factor**, as I define it, is *"taking the power in your life to become the entity that you want to become, and the ability* *to remove the barriers that block you or your positive currents, and stops you from doing just that, TRANSFORMING.* Moving away from the negative places, things, people and situations to the healthy, whole and positive person that is in the inside for you to become. It is the power to make changes in your life that cause you to reach self appointed goals of success, wealth, happiness and great lives. It is the power to **REACH** your thought out goals, hopes and happiness, to fulfill the dreams and promises you have made to yourself to succeed in this great life that God has given us to live, love and experience. It is the ability to live out the best life you can, to be in the abundance of presence of mind and thought of greatness, and an expectation of strength and power. It is the life Jesus Christ died for you to receive. A life of abundance, with nothing missing and nothing broken. This is the life of Transformation.

The factors that make up that life come from the many elements in our past, present and future experiences and how we choose to deal with them. How we respond to the choices life presents to us. How we live and how we pass our test in life. All these elements create our transformation and the factors that either add to us in a positive or take away from us in a downward spiral. Transformation is lived out by you. As we begin the journey of transformation we must first stop, sit back and do a brain scan of our past mistakes and realize what is holding us from being a better you. I propose for many of us that it comes down to one thing that we have failed to pass consistently. The area of distraction.

We have to want to pass, the **DISTRACTION TEST**. "This distraction test is the test that keeps you from embracing what you should be focused on, being the best person you can be, and helping others become that TRANSFORMED person as well." It keeps you distracted with time, energy, money and trials, so that your day is spent

You must begin this journey by making up your mind to pass the major test of life, it is called the "Distraction Test."

6

preoccupied with things that don't transform you.

I am so grateful for each person in this book who will share a small portion of their "transformation story" with you. Giving our life experiences can sometimes help others to overcome what you were able to make it through. When they see that someone just like them has taken on the same challenge and overcome them in victory. My life's testimony is poured out in the stories of these young men and women whom tell their trials in this book. I like to say, "truly been there, done that and more. I just didn't TALK the story, I have WALKED the story, wrote the book, make a tee Shirt, drunk a cup of tea, threw away the bag, and God gets all the GLORY!" So within them is a little of me, and then some. I truly know God will transform your life as well, if you are willing to **ADMIT IT** and **QUIT IT!** And put the Transformation Factors in process in your life, starting NOW.

You have to be intimate with transformation in your life to receive the benefits of the **POWER** to transform. We must gear up with everything within us to fight the good fight of faith. It takes a sincere level of faith to believe you can be better, and to really change negative patterns in the vicious cycles of defeat. This is what it will take to pass the distraction test.

First, take a deep breath, and decide you will have the determination to change. That you will not be distracted while you accomplish every task and factor that you need to reproduce in your new life of victory.

Some people fail in life because they get "older" but they didn't get better. They maintain a place of stagnancy for too long. They are here with you for a long time, but they don't get stronger. I/ we have to have a challenge in life not to only survive, but to thrive.

Most of our lives we have been told to do what it takes to just make it. However, we must transform our thinking to a pattern of **SUCCESS** to really be able to be **ALL** that the Creator intended for us to do and to be. We must make up in our minds that, "I don't just strive to get older and older, but I intend to get better and stronger. I want to reflect this in my mind, my spirit, my emotions, my physical, and of course in my financial gains. I want to get stronger in the things of the Lord. I want to be stronger in my thoughts and the patterns of my mind. I want to reflect this transformation power from the inside and let it transform me into the powerful creature that I was designed to be.

I hope this book will help you to become transformed and changed into a **POWER** source that God can use in the Kingdom and on the earth.

THIS BOOK CONTAINS 58 OF THE 89 TRANSFORMATION FACTORS. TO OBTAIN THE CONCLUDING FACTORS YOU MUST PURCHASE "IT'S ALL ABOUT THE KINGDOM" BY DR. J. G. RICE AVAILABLE AT YOUR LOCAL BOOKSTORE, ONLINE AT AMAZON.COM, OR CALL US AT 1-855-200-7729. YOU CAN ALSO VISIT OUR BOOKSTORE ONLINE AT WWW.KAWEBTV.COM

CHAPTER 1

"DISTRACTIONS"

Overcoming the distractions that hinder our transformation

The Distraction Test is the ability to overcome the forces that the enemy sends your way to disrupt you, dismantle you, and to side rail you from completing your ability to function; on the level that will cause growth, directional increase, and financial abundance in your life. While setting you back, spiritually, emotionally and socially.

Let's begin our journey by learning how to overcome the "Distraction Test."

It uses the force of "excuses and unfulfilled promises" to derail your daily thoughts and goals, until, weeks, months, and years pass... while you maintain your focus on other people and their thoughts, problems, and divisions . It causes you a lot of money time, and heart ache. .

Let's call it a **"Spirit of Distraction"** because it moves in time and seasons, and from person to person. It is demonic and it is sent out against the will of the creator God, to cause you ultimate failure .

To pass this test is to find out if you would recognize a demonic distraction for what it really is, and to be able to overcome it and move on successfully in your life. Can you recognize the devil for who he really is? Do you really know the devil's tricks? Or are you emotionally bound in a cycle of defeat by distractions that cause you not to transform to your beautiful place of rest, grace, peace and abundance?

I'm going to give you an example of something that really happened by way of church. It was sent to distract me from the real underlying problem. Understand, now that if you can see the **REAL** problems, not fake smoke screens, that you would move and respond differently. So, that's where deception must play a part in your life. If you could see Distraction dressed up in a label, you would probably avoid him. But Distraction comes in many shades of grey and colors. Bottom line, its task is to get you off purpose, waste a lot of time, money and life, that you will never recover. Many times the enemy uses camouflage to distract you from identifying the real problem or person causing the real problem.

Here's a story.... People will come into your life and say they want **"HELP"**, or they are supposed to help you. Or they go to a church and say they were **"SENT"** to that church/ ministry and that they are led there by God. Really, all you have to do is to watch the actions of people to know their real purpose in your life, good or bad. That's why I wonder sometimes when people say God plants them here (in the church) and they don't begin to change, they don't begin to grow, and their light bulb is not on. There is NO change to be seen in their lives, their appearance, nor their actions or ways. Then did God really send them to the ministry to be TRANSFORMED? Or did the devil send them to distract you? You have to ask the questions, and not be afraid of the answers.

And so I remember one time there were a couple of people that were here at Greater Harvest Christian Center Churches Worldwide- IGACCW (hereafter called Greater Harvest or GHCC) that were a part of the ministry, in body but never in spirit. They were ever so negative about everyone but their family or friends. One day out of the blue, they came early to church and said they wanted to "clean up the church" and had brought this "cleaning solution" with them that they said they wanted to clean up the church with it. They said they only used this one product because it was so good to clean up with. Then they said, "When you clean the church anything that has been put down that's not right the Lord is going to weed it out, root it out and it's going to leave." They said it was like Lysol/ Pine-Sol, but very strong. Well I just said, "Smells like Lysol, looks like Lysol. It's good to me."

Now they began to clean up the church and all of sudden we looked up and saw members beginning to leave. We didn't have but a few members left, and of course them. Each time a person left, they told me they were the **DEVIL**, until we were really scattered and did not have but a couple of members. We begin to go into prayer for membership restoration and after about three weeks the church was growing again. They were never happy with any new persons that came to the church, nor the old members that came back.

One day they ask me again to come in and clean out the church. I said with, a Holy Ghost unction, "No! I think I'm going to clean the church up this time." Isn't it amazing that God led me to use the same "cleaning supplies" that they had left from before. I began to spray in every corner and say, "God if any evil witchcraft of demonic forces or activity has been put down on the walls or in the corners, anything that we may not know about or may not see, root it out." Guess what? It wasn't a week and a half later that they up and left the church. See sometimes the main person that's trying to tell you who the witch is, is the witch themselves. They are trying to **distract you from seeing who they are**. To keep you in turmoil with others. To keep you in a box so you can't transform and see who they really are and cancel their assignment. People who distract you are often placed close to you, so they can keep tabs on you. So they can keep you off guard, unfocused, and unplugged into the correct people that God has assigned in your future. Those people that move you into your next level of accountability, which causes your own personal growth. These "distracting" people are assigned to try and delay or detour this connection.

I thought they were gone out of our lives, the cleaning

members of doom. However, to put the icing on the cake and really expose the devil for his plan of distraction, **God allowed them to be completely exposed as not being for us at all!** Months went by without hearing from them until we had the opportunity to go to court against someone that they (the former members) introduced us to earlier in their membership with the church. This person, tried to abuse the church finances. They lied about a service they did not complete and wanted us to pay for it. We refused and they decided that they were going to take us to court.

While he was trying to take us to court, the persons who were our former members, you guessed it, was there on their side! **You'll be surprised who's slivering up with people**. God said, "Watch this. I am going to show you who your enemy is/was right here in the flesh." They sat down laughing, giggling and plotting against us with smiles on their faces. They called themselves testifying against the church. You who once said you loved the church! Sitting with a sinner that you knew was wrong the entire time, because you were right in the middle of it all the time. You introduced us to this villain, schemer and trickster! By the way, need I say, **we won the case**. All praises go to God!

God will reveal to you your enemy. And even then you can't let this revelation of truth, regardless of who it comes with or who it causes to leave, cause you to fail the Distraction Test. Please don't let people distract you from greatness. Like Bishop Rice, our friend of the gospel Apostle Johnnie Clark (Rehoboth United Assemblies, Columbia, SC) and so many other great leaders have said, "Sometimes when people leave we clap our hands and say Praise God because He's doing the separation." And sometimes you have taken that attitude in your life. When people walk away from you that didn't mean you any good from the beginning, you can begin to rejoice in the Lord. You can begin to take heed in the Lord and say **"Thank You Jesus for your many Blessings."**

It's a blessing to get some people out of your life! God revealed to me the heart of the person 6 months before they were exposed in the natural. God will reveal to you who people are if you just look, listen and accept the truth of what you see. I saw this person about 9 months before they were revealed. I always pray for God to show me to ME and to show me any enemies, that I may know them as well, and be removed from their wicked devices.

So I dealt with that person, in the prophetic word of revelation that God gave to me, before they left. God allowed me to tell them one day out of the blue, "You have a stinky slick spirit." God already knew what He was saying. You have an undercover spirit. They were in denial responding, "How could you say that about me?" I could only reply, "Because it's true. God said you have a spirit of deception." I didn't know what God was saying, but God was protecting me from being distracted.

A True Prophet will see a lot of things and never tell it all!

I'll see you even if I don't say anything. If God doesn't release me to say anything, I'm not going to say anything. Sometimes God says, "Let the wheat grow with the tares." I recognize that when the enemy comes they are supposed to distract you from your next level in God. It's about wasting your time that you could have used for doing other positive things in God. I was supposed to be distracted by their friendliness, not to see the plan of the enemy to destroy the church. **The devil is SUBTILE**... The deflections that people bring into your lives can be planned for years, just to keep you distracted and not in transformation.

The point of being successful in your growth is knowing who the enemy is and how to deal with the enemy. If not, the enemy will distract you from your purpose and you will not pass the Distraction Test! You'll be so caught up in people and what they're caught in. You'll be so weaved in and around them, that when they snatched the brick out from under you, your whole building will fall if you're not carefully prayerful in God. When you refuse to be distracted then you are ready to be transformed. Transformation will come to those who expect it.

Let's do a football scene. Imagine a large man that's blocking your way, he's ready for action and he's focused. He's focused and he's looking at you, anticipating the fight. He's shielded himself up and he's ready for what's coming. You're trying to figure out a way to get around him or under him, but you see that he is on guard. He's not distracted, he's watching you. He's determining your moves and anticipating your play. He watching you and when you flinch he moves. When you bow, he bows. He lets you know that he's not afraid. You're not just going to take over. He's ready for the fight. But then on the other hand you see two or three guys that are supposed to be watching a special house, but they're just standing against the wall smoking cigarettes, laughing and are distracted by some little girl: **They are NOT fully on guard, and don't even see the danger ahead**, which is a person walking back and forth plotting how to get in, or break in and take the house valuables.

You know that they are distracted and that they're an easier mark! **READY FOR THE TAKING**! We have to be more aware to the tricks and traps of the enemy. As Bishop James Rice says here at Greater Harvest, "You have to put your mind on guard and put this visual scenario on your life. Begin to say, I must guard up these areas. I need to be blocking the devil." Be on Guard, not leaning against the wall being distracted. You need to know your purpose. You need to be focused because the enemy is like a roaring loin, he is seeking for whom he may devour. The power of defeating the attacks that come against you will only come in when you use your faith, heart and mouth. I have to use it and so do you! So in the "time of trouble" when the enemy wants to come in like a flood to attack you, he has to know that you are already on guard.

Overcoming witchcraft is easy. Just don't receive it.

I was telling somebody that the "witchcraft" was revealed to me in my sleep one night, when I saw the people involved were praying against my ministry and my marriage. WOW! You would not think that people would be so vicious, but they are! I saw some people, some I knew and some I did not, "praying" (a form of ungodly prayers) that demons of darkness be sent out to overtake me and smother the ministry from getting any light! But praise be to God who delivers us from the hand of the enemy. Who makes us known to the nations in a positive light and dispels the demons of darkness. We declare our Victory, our Oneness and our Success! *The BLOOD OF JESUS IS FOR US!*

"I overcome any witchcraft forces in Jesus Name. I crush the head of my enemies like a shaft in the wind and I send it back in Jesus name, as dust never to return to me or my generational line. That area is under the feet of the risen savior. Praise God from whom all blessing flow. Praise the Father, Son and Holy Ghost. I transform this situation that was sent for our bad and defeat, into the blessing and favor everlasting of God over our lives, all our members and partners lives and their families."

PRAYER IS STILL THE ANSWER! JESUS IS STILL THE ANSWER! And I don't know another answer!

God Gave me this victory prayer (You can use this prayer as well to break yokes in your life) as I woke up in the middle of the night and began to say, **"BOOMERANG! I SEND IT BACK!"** (Now you say these 5 power words until you feel the breakthrough.)

"BOOMERANG! I send back anything not for me, not like Jesus, or that is sent out against me or my family. I declare this right

NOW in the mighty name of JESUS . "BOOMERANG! I send it back! Every curse, every bad word, everything that's spoken against me and this ministry. I boomerang it! I send it back to the sender, in Jesus name. With no return to me or to my covered ones under the blood of Jesus ! May it wrap around your neck and drag you down, in the name of JESUS! You are not going to ride up in here Satan. Get out! You are put out, stumped out, casted out and will remain out.

There are no portal, no entries for you in my life. They are all sealed with the Blood of Jesus. Known and unknown. bad words from my enemies, are null and void, and boomeranged to the sender. I speak to the elements of time, season, future, and past, in Jesus name. Even what was thought of to be meant for bad has to yield itself to me a 50 fold trespass offering NOW in this season. I speak to seed, time and harvest. Come forth to me every good of the land in its season, and may every season in my life yield a bumper cargo of blessings. May they come in of constant yield and success. My light shines in darkness, and those stumbling will be glad for the light in my life to shine on them, that they may make their way to success. That they will bless me when they reach their goals. Mailbox MONEY is MINE!

Right NOW I demand repayment for any demonic interferences and spiritual delays caused by known and unknown sources of evil and despair. Now that you have been revealed, your access to my life, hopes, dreams, and path of success are denied. May you now be revealed by the atmosphere to those who war on my behalf. Be revealed NOW to everyone who wars against you on my behalf. You will be defeated by my angels who war on my behalf. The Spirit of the Lord is against you and I stand on the promises of God.

I am MORE THAN A CONQUEROR. The spoils belong to me for the sake of the King of Glory, the Lord Jehovah Sabboth, and the

Kingdom of GOD! I leave you no germination seed for replanting, I call crop FAILURE, FIRE and FLOODS on all ungodly works towards me and crush all negative seeds and mortify it. In Jesus Name!

I decree it is blown to the four winds of the continent and into Gods wind never to be assembled again, in the MIGHTY NAME OF JESUS! Defeat, Failure, and Bad news, I am not your Friend. I am a warrior in the Spirit and God grants me favor in every area of my life. I am "Happy, Healthy, Wealthy, and WISE (x7) .

I am Gods AMBASSADOR, transformed for His GLORY and His USE. Therefore my steps, my heart, my path, and future is wrapped and lined up in Him. I decree Victory to be Transformed into His very image TODAY in Jesus name!

So it is so for my Life and my Family, in Jesus precious, victorious, and triumphant NAME. His majesty reign FOREVER, and His mercies ENDURE forever.

I am using the Transformation Factor

This power prayer needs to be decreed, often over your life. Do not run from the Devil. Some people will run from the devil, instead of running the devil and his imps away from you, in Jesus name. I don't pick any fights, but I don't run from any either. I am guarding my spiritual place in God. Therefore I am alert and on guard in the place of readiness. I am using **The Transformation Factor** in my life to change things for me and my family. I know that it will work for you as well, if you use it.

Are you willing to Fight for your Transformation?

Sometimes all a person needs to know is that you are not afraid, not distracted, are armed for protection and willing to use your weapons of spiritual mass destruction. That you are willing to use whatever means necessary to protect whatever God has given you! Whatever necessary means to receive what God has for you. The question is, are you willing to **FIGHT** for your transformation? That's all the enemy needs to know. He doesn't like to pick on people who fight back. Once he knows you will fight for what God has for you , He will back down! But you can't just sit down and expect change to come. We have to be actively engaged in our victory, our success and our transformation!

The Stories / Testimonies, that you will read are about people just like you and I. People who became actively involved in their transformation, and begin to put into action the classes, seminars, teachings, principles and factors that were at hand to use. Including regularly attending church services, and becoming active in the worship of God ,which transforms your life. These factors along with the life changing principles from myself, Bishop James Rice and others (whom we have brought into their lives by the grace of God through Ministry and Mentorship), began to breathe a new hope into them. Now the sky and beyond is their new limit.

The Principles we teach weekly here at Greater Harvest Christian Center Churches Worldwide, an affiliate of the InterGlobal Association of Christian Churches Worldwide-IGACCW, are truly life changing. They are down to earth and practical application principles that if you put them into practice in your life you will transform in 11 months. One year from now, look at yourself, and you will see the difference in where you are, where you were, and where you came from. **APPLIED PRINCIPLES WORK !**

Become involved in "The Circle of Power" online and in person. Join a mentorship group and attend conferences. Some of you may need one-on-one counseling from your leadership, pastor, or personal counselor. **You may receive personal coaching from Arch Bishop James Rice, myself, Dr J. G. Rice, and the Team** and Leadership Staff, that is designed towards **TRANFORMATION, CHANGE and POWER for your life.**

There is no limit on the time factor as to when you can change. Do you have something you want to CHANGE? Then do it. Put the factors of transformation to work in your life. Put the **"58 Principles of Transformation to Success"** from this book to work in your life and start transforming today!

It doesn't take long to look back, and see steps forward !

Turn your life around!

It takes 30 days to gain a new habit!

Start today and be well on your way!

Complete the **"21–31 Day Turn Around Challenge"** to develop great habits by pushing yourself into something new! I assure you, that you will never be the same again. If you stop in the middle… START AGAIN. Just make up in your mind, if these people (and so many more) can change, then so can I!

Some of these persons are no longer in the ministry, because of their own choices, but we still love them dearly, and wish them the best on their path. Some are the stories are from young, old, male, females, singles, and married people that decided not to be distracted by the wrong compasses and to change their mindsets! The decision has to be made not to be distracted any longer from your **PROGRESSIVE ATTITUDE**. Not to be distracted by family, friends, circumstances, or themselves. But instead choose to follow the righteous faith of other **SUCCESSFUL PEERS**. These people who have changed their lives, they've followed the process. They have applied the transformation factors, the teaching and trainings to their lives. It's their stories, so receive it as such, the laughter, pain and the **TRANSFORMATIONS.** Within 11 months they were in an upward elevation! You too can be one of the people who change their lives in 11 months!

THE QUICK START PLAN!

We begin by using the Bible and we like to empower any new transformer with **Psalm 1.** This Psalm is one of our base transformation scripture and basic points. *"Get out of the council of the un-Godly, and into the council of the successful-Godly.* The faithfully wise. The kingdom keepers. The Christian Ambassadors. Those who have a track record of being and maintaining their salvation. Follow their faith. I cannot stress enough that you need a faith captain to help your transformation. Not just a person that talks about it, but "Be" about it!

Also understand transformation means change! And it may stretch you, deform the old you, expose parts you wanted hidden, recompose you, and create new functions in your life. If you want something new you've to do something different NOW! Do not think this book is for the unsaved person you may have brought it for! Truthfully, there are more deficient areas in the lives of the believer, as the lives of the unbeliever. The truth is our help is in the fact that the Blood of Jesus, His grace, and His mercy steps up for us so many times! So Christians need help as well. There are areas in our lives that we need help with, to break free from, and to transform. So these factors can help anyone who will admit to having about 3-4 areas that merit changing and in need of a transformation.

God wants the best for you. Can you get in agreement with God and want the best for yourself ?

If so, let's get ahead of next year, and use our 11 months to bring about these changes. You can't just sit there and pray and do nothing to change. Faith without works is DEAD! If so, let's go. I'll be your coach for the next 14 Chapters and 11 months. If you want to be a part of our online classes, just let me know! Contact my staff personally at ghccstaff.mm@gmail.com or visit www.chiefapostlerice.com.

To change the old, you have to **ADMIT IT** and **QUIT IT**. Oh yes, and please **DELETE IT**! Apostle Paul says in the bible, "Forget those things that are behind and PRESS towards the mark, of the HIGH CALL in Christ Jesus." No more delays, lies, or denials. If you want better then it's time to change. Take the "21-31 day" challenge found in this book and use the tools to Transform. Transformation time is now! The Transformation Factor lies within you!

CHAPTER
2

The
"Spirit of Ratism"

Identifying And Overcoming the "Spirit Of
Ratism" That Keeps You From Transforming

Unblocking The Portals That Block My Transformation

Unto your Glory, Lord Jehovah Tsidkenu, your anointing is upon us. The word of the Lord for his people prophetically for transforming is Isaiah 42. As I was just Worshipping (Our God) He gave me Isaiah 42. God said, "Get this word to my people forever."

Thus said God the Lord, "He that created the heaven and stretch them out, He that spread forth the earth and that which cometh out of it; He that giveth breath into the people upon it and spirit to them that walk there in: For I the Lord have called thee in **righteousness**. And I will hold thy hand and will keep thee; and I will give thee for a **covenant** for the people, for a light of the gentiles." I've been given his anointing because of Faith for a covenant. When God makes a deal with you He will not break it. He will back it up. When God makes a deal with you He doesn't break his part. That's what covenant means.

Sometimes when things aren't working like you want them to work or like you think they should to work, you want to back off your end of the covenant. God said, "I gave you for a covenant to the gentiles," to the believers. **You are the light that they're going to see. You are the one that's going to show that God can work it out.** That's why you'll hear me sing, "Didn't He say He'll work it out!" No matter what you're going through, "Didn't He say He'll work it out?" If you just hold on to His hand, if you just keep the faith and keep your flesh down, "Didn't He say that He would work it out?"

God can work it out!

Right when you were about to give up, "Didn't He work it out?" Right when you were about to throw in the towel, "Didn't He work it out?" Didn't He do that before? What would make you think He wouldn't do it again? **HE WILL DO IT AGAIN!** He says, "I will give thee for a covenant for the people, for the light of the gentiles." I'm so glad God gave me as a covenant. My purpose is to open up blinded eye, so the blind can see. Now sometimes you have to teach the blind by Braille so they can see. Sometimes you can give a blind person glasses, and they can see. Sometimes you have to give them a Seeing Eye dog so they can see. But no matter what it takes, I want you to see. Some people have to have surgery. They have to get the cataracts removed from their eyes to see. Some people have to use magnifying glasses to see. But the blind eyes can see.

He said, "I will give thee a light of the gentiles to open the blind eyes; to bring out the prisoners from prison." It doesn't refer only to those behind prison bars. You can be imprisoned in your mind. When it's your mind that is locked up, you're in prison and you need a **Transformation.** When you are locked up in your mind, you have to be ready to be free when your sentence is over. You must be ready at all cost to Go! You've been released by the blood of Jesus, NOW GO!

I gave a scenario about little rats living in a cage. And how those rats, once they've been trained, won't go but so far. I don't care how much you open that door, the rats has been trained and will refuse to exit out. Some of you have that same "limited rat mentality." God wants to bring you out from the prison of your **"Ratism".** Ah, that's a new word. God wants to bring you out of your Ratism. Hallelujah! God wants to bring you out of that mentality. He wants to take you from the prison of limitations. The prison of your past. The prison of your own self destruction. The rat trap and the rat race that goes nowhere fast. God gives you a leader to bring you out of prison. Leadership is for the followers. Leadership does not stop at the leader. God's Word says, "As it is in the head so shall it be in the body." **So as I'm anointed to bring you out, you should to be able to bring someone else out of something.** Even if it's telling someone you want to help change, "Just come out of profanity and speak better with your words and the precious tongue God gave us all. We can change the world one word at a time!"

God gives us leaders to shine light on our darkened lives

You're anointed! God gave me the anointing to push the door open and bring out the prisoners from the prison and them that sit in darkness. **Although the lights are on, some people are sitting**

28

in darkness. God gave your leaders to you, to help you come out of the darkness. Sometimes you come out of the darkness by paying your light bill company. Sometimes you have to light a candle until you can get the money. Even the small light of a candle can change things, and the darkness has to leave. Sometimes you may just need a little flashlight. But whatever it is, God has sent somebody in your Life that can help you come out of darkness. Notice God says "darkness," but you're still in the prison house. So not only are you in prison, you're in a dark prison. This is so with those who refuse to transform. They're in prison and in the darkness! They're confined in the darkness of their soul and in the natural darkness of your environment. We must have a Transformation factor in our lives and believe in the power through Jesus Christ to **CHANGE.** To make a light come on. St. Matthew said in his writings, "You are the Light of the World, ...a city set on a hill."

DO NOT HIDE YOUR LIGHT!

God sent people to help you keep your light shining. The Apostle, the Prophet, the Evangelist, the Pastor, and the Teacher. Each part having its intricate place and purpose in your life. All five make up a hearty healthy meal. The meat, rice, sweet corn, potatoes and gravy. Gravy by itself just wouldn't make a meal. You would be malnourished with just gravy and wouldn't grow. You would be sickly and stuck! **Every form of teaching has its place and should be embraced as a gift from GOD!** You must have that meat & potatoes to appreciate the gravy. The gravy by itself just won't do. So you have to want the truth, the staples of the meal, not just a bunch of sweets to eat. Sweets do not help you transform. Good sound teaching and mentorship will help you transform. So God sends the 5 fold ministry to help you come out. "Come Out" is the cry from your soul. You have to come out of Ratism!

Many come out of Egypt, but Egypt did not come out of them! They took the same problem to a new place!

Can you quit being a rat? Aren't you tired of just cheese? Peanut butter still brings you into the same trap every time? We need God to help produce the transformation factor in our lives. "I am the Lord, that is my name, and my Glory will I not give to another." He's talking about helping you come out, going into Him, transforming, and giving Him the Glory. Salvation comes from God. **Salvation means to be rescued.** WOW! God wants us to be rescued! That's a fact! Honestly, I've been walking with God and saved by his Son Christ Jesus a long time. However, I don't have any salvation for you. It's not mine to give! I can only lead, you like any other good disciple, to the SAVIOR. JESUS is his name.

Jesus is the answer, and I don't have another answer!

I can teach you about salvation, but you have to receive it. Then you have to live it after you get it. I can tell you what salvation looks like. I can tell you what salvation is not. **I can tell you what salvation is because I've been saved long enough to know what it is to be saved.** I can tell you when God is working on you and when you're struggling. Why? Because we have been there, done that, wore the T-shirt, washed it till it faded then threw it away. I've been broken, just not in three places. I've seen lighting flashing and heard thunder rolling. I didn't create the Heavens, but I can tell you what it takes to get there. I didn't create Hell, but I can tell you what it takes to miss it. At this season in our walk with God, Bishop James Rice (my husband) and myself, we know what we are called to do and feel like we are finally doing it because we have embraced our purpose! I know who I am, whose I am, and what I am. **I am a Kingdom AMBASSADOR!** I've been sent to set the captives free! I can help you, but only if you want transformation.

Let's talk frankly. If I let you out of jail and you tell me, "I like jail, and I want to go back," that's probably where you will end up, no matter what I say and do. You'll probably fight me tooth and nail to go there! So I would be wasting the precious fuel of the Holy Spirit to drive you somewhere you don't want to go. Yes, I could force you to go and be there, but you'll run away as soon as your feet hit the ground! A waste of energy on my part. So I pastor those who want me to pastor them. I mentor those who want me to mentor them. I pray for those who want me to pray for them. I help to transform them that want to be **TRANSFORMED!** Those who want to stay on the Hamster Wheel, I understand. I will watch you run your race until you yield or die, knowing one day you will SUBMITT to the will of God.

How many people do you know have been to jail? When they were released did they say, "I want to stay here with my friends?" Well then, **when God sets you free, why are you always trying to hold on to what was in jail?** Trying to hold on to the "Ratism." When you're let out of jail you leave everything there. You are not trying to take any bags. No one is thinking, "I need my prison soap" or "I need my prison tissue." No one goes back for a missing sock. No one says, "Wait I left something in prison. I got to go back and get it." When you leave there you're not looking back. When certain people see you on the street that you were in jail with, you don't even try to identify with them. You want to leave it all behind you. No one wants to continue their affiliation with a scarred past. So you won't even hang out with known felons. You'll get new friends and do positive things. It should be the same when you come out of the prison of your mind, the **"Prison of Sin"** and get free in Jesus.

So I must ask the question. **Why is it when God gets you out of sin you're still hanging out with known sinners?** How is it when God brings you out of the crack house, you keep going back to the crack house? Your thoughts I'm sure are pure. You think you can "save others while you are still wet from the waters of sin yourself." You may even say, "I'm just going back over there to get somebody saved." You would not go back to the prison to get them save. Especially if you had to do additional prison time to do it. Some things you run to, and some things you run from. It will save your very life and keep you renewing your **MIND in CHRIST!**

Everyone can see the rat in you.

The truth is the mindset of returning to the things that have you, or had you bound is " Ratism." **Only a rat keeps returning to the hole, to the sewer and to the mess it's made.** To be transformed you must ask yourself, what is in you? Sometimes we have become desensitized to what people really do see about us. Don't be like others who do not care if everyone can see they are a rat. Do not allow yourself to show your Ratism all over. You are empowered to change your ways and transform. A rat will get wet and run through the streets squealing and dripping filth EVERYWHERE. Naked and not ashamed, spreading diseases. Ratism tells a size 24 person to put on a size 12 with no underwear and walk the streets. Squealing, dripping filth, with a lack of class and purpose. If your body doesn't fit it, quit it or supersize it!

Justified Ratism

Some of us have Justified Rats. We will pray for a problem to leave and continue to bring it into our life. You accept your rat as a **PET**. You brought a cage, a little turn around thing, and put it in there and called it a Hamster. But it's still a Rat! We accept our problem and want everyone else to accept it. You're running around talking about, "look at my Hamster." No, you have a Rat. You have a justified rat. You don't want to let it go. **So instead of getting rid of it, what you do is dress it up.** You make it convenient. But at the end of the day you're still a rodent. You still have ratism.

Once a Rat, always a Rat, no matter what we call it !

It's hard to get of a rat, but it can be done! There's not much you can do with a rat, but Ratism can change. The Glory of God has come to pull us out of these prisons. The Glory of God has come to pull us out of Ratism. The Glory of God comes to say, "Why are you acting like a Rat when you really a Lion?"

A Rat and a Lion have different territories and different characteristics. Even though they're on all four, fuzzy and furry, they are two totally different species. God has called you to have dominion with authority. Yet you are acting like a sewer rat. May I go deeper? A rat with your secret sins, with an attitude, and with characteristics flaws. **You will not grow up and become a lion when you're too busy trying to hold on to being a Rat.** God has sent me, and other Kingdom Ambassadors in the 5 Fold Ministry to say, "Hey! You are acting like a Rat! But you look like a Lion. What's your problem?" I've come to set the captive free! "For I will do a New Thing," says the Lord, "A new thing do I declare." To come to the new thing go to Isaiah 40, starting at verse 3. He says, "Make straight in the desert a highway for our God. Every valley shall be exalted, and every mountain and hill shall be made low. And the crooked shall be made straight and the rough place shall be made smooth. And the Glory of the Lord shall be revealed.

Let the GLORY of the LORD rise among US!

God will only get the glory out of you when you become balanced. Your high place must come down and your low place must come up. Your crooked ways have to be made straight if you want the Glory of God to be revealed in your Life. That's what Isaiah is saying. **God wants to transform our life Highways!** There are some things in you that have to balance out. The high places have to be brought down! The low place in your life have to be brought up. How do you bring them up? You can't bring them up by yourself.

God said, "I will send thee," someone to set the captives free from high mindedness and Ratism. He can balance out your day, balance out your life, and balance out your future. Some of you will delay getting to your future, because you can't let go of the Ratism from your past. **TRANSFORM** from this thought! God said, "every valley has to be brought up." That means every low thing in my life, God must deal with that. God will deal with some of your lowliness, your nastiness, your despicable ways, your cantankerous mindset, your untrustworthiness, and your unfaithfulness. God will deal with your insecurities. God must deal with all of that low stuff. God will deal with you thinking more highly of yourself than you really are. The high place must come down. None of us really want to admit that's in us, but that's what we must transform from. We must come out that stuff.

I can fly like an Eagle because I am one!

Now you say, "I can't do it by myself." That's why God sends Leaders to get in our stuff. Because we will not admit to our

Ratism until the leader says, "You're a rat!" Let me show you a picture of the ratism, "it's you!" **You didn't know you were a chicken until you looked up saw an eagle flying.** You didn't know you weren't supposed to eat dirt and worms, until somebody gave you some fresh tuna. An eagle eats fresh tuna, he doesn't eat dirt and worms. You didn't know that you were supposed to be eating sushi, the finer things in life. You didn't know that because you were too busy clucking dirt like a chicken. Until somebody came and said, "Hey! Why are you in this coop? Get yourself out this coop! You don't have any business in this coop! You are an Eagle! What are you doing in a coop with a bunch of chickens? **WHATS YOUR PROBLEM?** Transform yourself and become who you already are! Open the door and get out! Now that you know better, do better. Go and fly! Don't be foolish. Transform now and fly! No more excuses. No one that we've ever mentored thought on the first meeting they could change, but by the second meeting they knew they could change, and wanted to **TRANSFORM!**

You're like the chicken in the coop. Instead of you leaving the chicken coop, you go and round up all the chickens and go pecking the person that's trying to get you out of the coop of sorrow, misery, and despair. So unfair! Finding other rats to run with is easy. Just like Bishop Rice says, "You'll go and call around until you find somebody to agree with your foolishness." That's so much easier than changing. Every chicken in the coop with you will always say, "Why leave the coop, we will be dinner anyway." Every eagle will always tell you to fly! Don't be dinner today. Live another day to produce an egg. **Strengthen your wings and FLY** the next time the door of life brings you an opportunity! Don't say NO… just FLY!

How do we get to know the songs we hear? We begin to sing them!

You're going to sing your song, negatively or positively, until you get somebody that knows the chorus. You're going to get somebody in agreement with your clucking and your pecking to keep you as a chicken. Instead of them telling you to get up and be the great eagle you can be. People that can see an eagle in you have great faith. They sing a different song, **"I believe I can fly. I believe I can touch the Sky...."** If your leader says you're an eagle, then they must think you can fly. So take a chance and flap your wings! I know that you've never been an eagle before, but you're an eagle now. So do it! Just try and take off the ledge. But before you leap, get a flying coach! Wait on someone to teach you how to use those wings that you've never use before. Don't be afraid because you haven't been an eagle before. The only thing you've ever been was a chicken afraid to transform!

The only thing many of us have ever been was a rat. I meet people that are often over 30 and don't know how to balance a checkbook. That don't know how to be a **SEED KEEPER!** They were used to bouncing checks, spending everything, and being broke. They became experts at jumping from bank to bank, because many of us had a "broken financial" mentality. Now we must transform immediately, for the sake of our future generation and ourselves. Rats eat everything, but an eagle and an ant store up. A rat will eat everything until it burst, never worrying about tomorrow or making any plans on saving. The Holy Ghost comes to move in, but you'll kick him out and keep being a rat.

Let me expose "Ratism" to you

Sometimes when you're in a mist of rats, and you being the lion (Different, Strong, Valiant, Bold and on your way to Transformation), rats will try and gang up on you. **You can't rest with rats, because when you wake up they will have eaten your eyeballs out.** Rats eat their own, eat its children and everything. Get a little sore on you and a rat will chew you until the only thing left is your you bone. A rat will eat a Lion if there's enough of them and if that lion is wounded. Let me share a true story with you. The names have been changed to protect the feelings of the head rat.

One night in bible study we discussed that God makes it clear that He doesn't hear a sinners prayer. It says, "for we know that God doesn't hear a sinners prayer but only hear the righteous." The bible also says that if you act like a fool, in the day of your calamity, when you call upon him, he's going to laugh at you. The bible also says that you cannot do whatever you want to do and still make it to heaven. **Only the righteous shall see God.** If you don't live righteous and are playing with God, when you need him He will withdraw His hand from you. That's the same thing all the way round. In my interpretation, God says, "to all that don't want to change, if you act like a sinner then go to your father the devil and get what you need." We also discussed that the scriptures says that everybody is not a child of God. God created us all, but we chose our own paths, destiny and ways of our fathers! That's why the bible says, "You are of your father the devil." **The devil has children!** All who follow him and refuse to live the Christian life styles are the devils children! He's the author and the father of lies. He's a big RAT and you are a RAT. The only time God hears a sinner prayer is for the prayer of repentance unto salvation. I don't care what you thought. He rains on the just and the unjust. Just because you got in trouble and you said, "Oh Lord help me" and you got out, doesn't mean God did it. The devil could have gotten you out to set you up to do it again so you can be locked up for life! If we profess the word of Salvation and wear a cross, we must transform to live right to impress our savior. I'm talking about you having a life line legacy of learning to love God enough to transform your life to holiness. This transformation factor will keep you out of Ratism.

So that was our powerful bible study lesson that night! People were freed, saved, and delivered that night. TRANSFORMATION began in the lives of the new babes in Christ! But some of the people who were in church that night got upset with the word of God. **Rats cannot accept the truth of the word, it is like poison to them!** So the Rats had a meeting after church. They gathered in the sewer (living room) to have a meeting with the Head Rat who told the other little Rats that it's alright for you to be a rat. God knows your heart and what the pastor said was not right. We all God's children. The Head Rat also told the little Rats, "It doesn't take all of that to go to heaven. God knows your heart." The question arose as to moral standards by one of the little Rats. She was told that it was alright to continue in an affair and taking the married man's money, and any other man's money that is stupid enough to give his money to her. Now this came from the Head "Missionary" Rat. A so called grandmother " Minister" speaking with her grandchildren "church goers" and counseling them to participate in adultery and justifying it as God won't care.

You have to be a Rat stuck in Ratism to tell your conclave of Rats to take another Rats cheese. Even rats have respect for other rats. So of course, this here Rat is the Head RAT, and has been a RAT, and knows how to be a RAT. All she can give out is Rat poop. Ratism!

You have to change who you eat with. You have to change who you meet with. You have to change what kind of information is coming to you because it will create Ratism in you. **When the truth comes, you'll reject the truth and believe a lie because of Ratism!** That Chicken Coop Mantality. I don't care what the title is behind their name. "Grandma Rat, Mama Rat, Auntie Rat or Uncle Jed Rat! Any preacher that will tell you to not believe the word of God, so they can get whatever they want to get from you is a Rat! Preacher Rat!

Sometimes when you're in the midst of Rats you have to run.

The Rat meeting concluded with all the Rats trying to eat the Lion. The person that was telling them that they need to do right and transform. All the Rats started running up the Lions back and up his legs and biting him. The lion had to get out of there. In the midst of Rats you have to run. **You have to go least they eat your destiny. Least they eat up your future. Least they eat up your purpose.** Least they start to run up your nose and eating up your brain cells. Leave those Rats alone, leave those chickens alone. Leave those mindless people alone. **TRANSFORMATION IS YOUR FRIEND!** I want to be with people who are not rats. I purpose to be rat and roach free! I don't want to be associated with them. I've come to a point in my life, in my ministry, in my oneness and in my mindset to leave the rodents of life alone.

Why must I have this change? So glad you want to know! Because while I'm sleeping, I can't have a rats wondering around in my brain trying to eat up the goodness in me. ***Ratism is wrong***. Identify it, cancel the assignment, and don't accept it. Because you have hung out and fed the rats for so long, transforming will require you to kill the rats to remove them from your destiny! Just realize a rat is toxic and leaves a lot of poison.

This has been a light happy chapter, and you may have laughed at a lot the examples. But it has a lot of meaning to it. Don't let the laughter fool you. Now let's deal with the hidden Ratism.

Hidden Ratism...DEAL OR NO DEAL!

Understand friends, that your surroundings can cause your mind to revert to something you should not be. If you don't intend to be a Rat, then stop hanging out with them. **DEAL!** When God is looking at you He sees a LION, so you need to get rid of those tendencies in you that causes you to act like a rat. **DEAL!** Stop acting like a chicken. Be anything but a chicken. Be a dove, be a raven, or be a sparrow. Be somebody that moves upward, and does not keep going back to the same old thing. "WOW" Even a duck moves from pond to pond. **DEAL!** I'm not talking about jumping all around from place to place. Be Progressive in your mind. Seeing things that cause you to be better.

Be anything but a Chicken, unless you want to be on the Dinner Table of Life!

Other than people on the farm, you're not going to walk into many people houses and just see great big beautiful pictures of chickens on they're walls. You may see swans, doves, sparrows, eagles but you are not going to see a Michael Angelo painting of chickens. You are not going to walk in anyone's living room and see a big "rat collage" painting. But you'll see lions, tigers, bears and deer's. If you're going to be something in life let your value increase. **DEAL!** Learn how not to become the problem, but the problem solver. This is what God is requiring for his Glory. You have to straighten those crooked ways out.

Do you believe that you have some crooked ways that has to

be straightened? Do you believe you have some high places that need to be brought down? Do you believe that you need to be more balanced in your life? Great! So I receive this word even for myself. You have to be in balance, God is causing you to be balanced so His glory can rest on you. Not just come and go, but so that His glory can rest on you. And that's where I'm trying to get you to, the place where His glory can just rest on you. To rest in your life, as you transform. **DEAL !**

When the real glory comes into your life, (not just those friends that wants to boost you up... **NO DEAL**!) Everybody will know. True miracle's signs and wonders will follow you. And all flesh shall see it. I want to be not a "Glory Chaser, but a Glory Carrier." **I don't want to always be chasing after God. I want Him to be with me. Dwelling and abiding in ME!** I want to catch up with the presence of God and carry His glory in my life!

Checks and Balances

For the mouth of the Lord has spoken it. This is a Prophetic Word. Him that has an ear for transformation, let him hear what the spirit of the Lord is saying to the church. He's saying, "time to balance out." You have to bring your life to a balance. **The checks and balances in your life have to match on a consistent basis**. That's how God gets the Glory. If I come to you one time with a problem and you talk about me, the next time I see you I want to pray for you. Then the next time you want to curse me out for no reason. You're not balanced. You're all over the place. **NO DEAL!**

You have to be consistent in the way you're handling things. You have to know when your season of trying to help a rat is over. Because if you keep that rat to long, you'll make him a pet and that's something within yourself. You have to know when to let go of something within yourself that is causing you to be a Rat or a Rat Lover! Or you'll become comfortable when **that season needs to be over!** You just need to be over with that. That's why God says, "Greater is He that is in you." The lion is in you. Let the lion live so the rat will die. The eagle is in you. Let the eagle live so the chicken can die. You have to make a decision to be a winner or to live defeated. You can't be both. You can't be a lion and a rat. You can't be an eagle and a chicken. Something has to die so something else can live. Choose this day whom you will serve. The eagle or the chicken? The lion or the rat? You choose. The decision is yours. What are you going to be in your spirit? What are you going to transform to?

What kind of animal are you?

You've looked in the mirror long enough and saw the chicken and the rat. Time for you to look and see an eagle and a lion. Time for you to see something that God sees, that God wants to use. Whatever you choose to be, understand that's a decision you have to live with. At the end of the day, God is going to tell you if you have been a good and faithful servant. When the bible lines up and tells you, you have not been good and faithful, are you going to be like those with the ratism and try to justify your foolishness? Because what the rat really says is, "I don't care what they say, I believe what I want to believe." The rat says, "I went and asked another preacher if God hears a sinners prayers." And because that preacher is a Rat, that preacher says, "Yes." But it's in the Bible, and it will not change no matter how many meeting you have nor how many rats you gather! **NO DEAL!**

That's why my bible tells you and I to study to show ourselves approved. Don't you believe those lies that the rats are telling you. It's a bad seed to listen or believe that heresy. You cannot live your life any kind of way and still go to heaven. That will not happen. **NO DEAL!**

Heaven is a prepared place for a prepared people. You would have stripped yourself down here and made these crooked ways straight. That's the qualifier. So are you qualified to go to heaven? Repeating a salvation prayer, then going back out into the world and doing everything you want to doesn't qualify you. Why? Because you said it with your mouth, but your heart never changed. Your ways never changed. *"Be ye not conformed, but be ye transformed by the renewing of your mind." (Romans 12:2)* You're so far from God, as the east is from the west. God will say, ***"Depart from me, I never knew you. You worker of inequity."***

(Matt 7:23) But I cast out demons in your name many will say. You still were a worker of iniquity, because in your heart and by your ways, you refuse to change. So boost yourself up! Don't let your Ratism fool you! Please don't let it fool you into thinking you don't have to change. The change has to start in your heart. The word says, *"Out of the abundance of your heart your mouth speaks." (Luke 6:45)*

Just Quit It!

Think on these things and ask yourself, what kind of ratism am I involved in? What things that deny and detain me from really doing better? Do I need to void out of my mind and circle? What are these things holding me back from being greater than I am right now? What do I need to get out of me? What kind of hamster ways do I need to let go of? Running around in the same old circle, just enjoying the same old sin. Get off the wheel, wake up and progress. Some rats don't even get off the wheel to sleep. They just sleep right there and wake up running into that same sin, the same problems, and the same cycles. The door is open, you don't have to stay in the prison. God sent someone to open up the blinded eyes. If stay unchanged it's because you want to. There is no sin that deep that you just can't stop doing. Nike says, "Just do it!" I say, "Just Quit It!" We really do what we want to do, and we justify the rest. We are strong in our minds and in our spirits. *"We can do all things through Christ who strengthens us." (Philippians 4:19)*

The prayer of deliverance from Ratism

If you really want the glory, like I want the glory of God to be with me, you'll ask the Lord of the harvest to straighten some things out. Like Bishop James Rice (my husband) says, " Take a Spiritual Flush." Sometimes you have flush some stuff out. What we may stand up and say out of our mouths on stage, we can't live it out behind closed doors. This should be our prayer of deliverance and transformation.

Let's Pray...

Straighten my crooked ways Lord. Bring the highs down and bring the valley up. Help me Jesus, so that your Glory can stay in my life. God, I need your help. Jesus be my help, because that's all I saw, that's all I know. Help me Lord. I'm going to kill my own destiny and kill my own future if I don't lose this ignorance. If I don't lose this Rat mentality. Oh Father, I need you to take it out and I need to stomp on it and keep it out. Lord take it out! Give me a spiritual laxative. Least I continue with my Ratism. Least I continue as a Chicken in the dirt plucking for worms until the day I die and am eaten up and forgotten.

I'm reading the word God, but I apply it to others. Help me to apply it to myself. Least when I preach to others I become a cast away myself. Oh Father, before you strengthen me, remove the bad stuff. Strip it out! Strip it out! Strip it out Lord! Everything that is not like you God, those things that I know are not like you God. Strip that foolishness out of me. I renounce my own self. I renounce how I let the devil use me. Sabotaging my own destiny Lord. Help me Father. God I have to Spiritually flush some stuff out of me. The truth is what I declare in the open, I have major struggles with in private. I want everyone to think I am more prepared to fight this spiritual battle than I really am. I find myself wanting to go backwards instead of coming forward. I find myself wanting to go back to the old, back to that death trap. Back to the Rat life!

But God, instead let me be an eagle and rise above these setbacks and unfulfilling ways, so that I may fly high. Maybe someone, while in their chicken stage, will look up for a brief moment in time and see me flying higher in you. Soaring like an eagle. Let them see my light shining and may it bring to them the "Hope of Glory" so that they may know that they too can fly. May my awakening and progress cause a change in their hearts and minds towards a new destiny. Most of all, let me be that eagle. The first eagle they've ever seen in their lives, family and job soaring so high. Let them never forget seeing this eagle soar, and want to flap theirs wings and join me at the TOP!

My Father, El Shadai, please help me to transform, in Jesus name. El Jireh, help me to transform to a higher place in you! El Shalom please bring me up in the TRANSFORMATION FACTOR of my mind, in Jesus name ! Thank you El Nissi, I praise you for delivering me, from ME. O praise you for giving me the power to Change.

Prayer Partners

If you have not done the **31 days to Transformation, Change and Power** chapter, let's begin to do it today. Let's take one thing, and focus on it, and purpose to change that one thing within 31 days, beginning today! Today in the mighty name of Jesus, and know I am with you.

+ meetings, "Circle 59" meetings, or "Circle of Power" meetings!

Let's get started towards your transformation TODAY!

CHAPTER 3

THE TRANSFORMATION FACTOR

31 DAYS TO A TURN AROUND

If you are reading this chapter it is because you have discovered that you need a "turn around" in an area of your life, there is something you wish to change, delete or to add to your life walk and you wish to embrace and take the time to do it NOW! That's great we all need to improve in some areas or to strengthen in some areas of our lives.

It is said to take at least 28-31 days to break any habit, or to make a new change. I believer that positive confessions and speaking to a things also helps you to refocus and to bring better images into your head, heart and way of thinking. These things that you speak or mediate on will give you the poser to refocus.

To really have the power to turn around or to "Change", we must know that God has the best in mind for us and for our lives, Plans to prosper us and to bring us to a joyous end. It is often our folly or lack of determination to progress in a positive mode that will create for us holes of failure, that we seem to always drop in!

We want you to stay ur of those deadly dark holes and to live by the springs of living water in your life.

So here we go…. TO begin to Transformation in any area of our lives there are 5 vital steps. But we will start with step one.

NUMBER 1 : ADMIT IT, You must admit you have a circumstance, situation, problem, challenge or Thing that you realize MUST CHANGE –TRANSFORM to really be the "Full Successful Person" you were created to be ! ADMIT IT, say the problem and lets work on one or TWO things at a time.

NUMBER 2: BE REALISTIC with CHANG, we may need all 11 months to work on most of our problems especially if you have more than 5 things you would like to change or become better in.

Let's be realistic; these areas did not get bad overnight, so you must go through the process in every area and expect God to fix them as you give him permission and access to do so. He the Holy SPIRIT and your Coach will not fight you to change, you must be willing to TRANSFORM.

Number 3: PREPARE TO QUIT IT! Yes you must prepare to STOP the behavior that has led to your demise. A lot of areas were created for you or to you, HOWEVER you created a lot of area of failure as well, These things and habits, you must be prepared to quit. Yes if you want to stop smoking, you have to quit buying what your smoking. and refuse anyone to give you items you NO LONGER TRULY WANT. To prepare to **QUIT negative behaviors** you must also be willing to sever yourself from environmental influences that YOU KNOW breed and create the holes that cause you to fall. So you must make an honest assessment as to WHAT pulls you to the negative behavior you are desiring to put out of your life.

Number 4: IT'S TIME TO GET SPECIFIC , Make a list, of Items you plan to loose from your life, things to be turned around from , List all the times you want to turn around from, from the most needed to the lesser needed, write down all the things you need to quit doing to become a more productive person. Then identify why you do these things to yourself, or allow yourself to become involved in all "bad behaviors". These are the forces that will hold you in the hole, (the negative forces). Now List and positive things you plan to replace them with TURNED AROUND TOO (thing that will help you to come out of the hole) this is your ladder to TRANSFORMATION AND TURN AROUND, this is your POSITIVE FORCES that will help you to change and to go into better areas in your life.

Number 5: GET SOMEONE TO HELP YOU, Become Accountable to your decisions, tell someone that **you will allow** to hold you accountable to your need to change and embrace the new you, that you are trying to become. Tell them to be tough on you , because you really want to change, Ask them to report you to another person you feel accountable to if you become nonresponsive to them, and Prepare yourself for a Real Transformation.   The accountability person should not be someone, or anyone you are in the same "rut" or situation with; Try your Pastor, your Mentor, your Coach, your Director, your Supervisor, or a Person you hold in high regard. They as well should be a Christian who can "Pray" with you and Pray for you as well. This journey can seem short or long depending n how your mindset is towards change; But it can be done! Let's begin to work on one, or two things at time; and before you know it you will be better tomorrow than you are today!

YOU must PRAY the PRAYER everyday at least 2 times a day for the most positive results!

Why pray this prayer at least 3 times a day for the 28-31 days? It will help to keep you focused and to created a place of balance in you, towards the things you are praying to change. You must CALL OUT THE AREA OF CHANGE TO ARE PRAYING ABOUT, and mentally get in your mind a picture of what.; and What you what to change,. As well you need to know how you want it to change, and what you are going to replace the old habits with new positive ones. Yes you have to have a picture of what to replace it (bad stuff) with (New Positive Stuff). Do not skip a Day make time to pray and confess positive over your life, NO ONE ELSE is responsible for creating GOOD for you but YOU! This is another areas you must transform your thinking in, believing that it is someones else's fault or responsibility ! No its yours, so lets get to work on it! NOW ! lets begin our TRANSFORMATION NOW ! RIGHT now!

OK What is it you want to TRUN AROUND ?

Let's think about it now and lets prepare to get to work , You will need some items listed below to help you in this journey, If you don't have them it's ok, make use of what's around you and the end result will still happen for you!

What will I need to make this process Successful

You will need to get and keep up with a 28-31 day calendar (one year) if you are on the 11 month program to change several things in your life ! So let's get a CALENDER, **a large one** to track your change. At the beginning of the 28-31 days write what you are working on in the calendar! That Step one; (you can buy a calendar at a dollar store (or make one in your journal book).

Get or make a journal book, this is a notebook of any kind, that you can write in.

Find the scripture in the list in this book that you are going to read for the day; Then Write your scripture for the day on the calendar as well, as in your journal… (after you have read it). Also write in your journal what it means to you and how you are going to change it to transform yourself.

Now "Pray your Prayer" today and believe that you will apply good principles in your life to keep the negative habits and forces away from you. Believe you will make good choices and better selections to help you become a better person in life.

When you begin to pray your prayer it may seem long but go through it you need everything it says to your life to CHANGE and TRANSFORM!

After a couple of days the prayer will seem short and only take less than 30 minutes of your day to pray. Finally find you a positive SONG to play after you pray every day and sing that song whenever you think on any negative thing, to pull your mind back to prayer and that fact you are changing from the old going to the new !

Bishop James Rice our Archbishop is a prayer warrior and has people praying for you, as you are committed to change, we want to know your name to pray more effectively for you, go to WWW.BISHOPPRAY.COM, and let us know, you are trying to make a TURN AROUND Transformation ! and we will add your name to the list of prayer as well.

Most Importantly, Speak FAITH ! don't talk NEGATIVELY 1 , Change your negative influences and get involved in positive activities, like Church, or other social service projects. I believe in you, and these persons in this book went through the same process, IT IS WHAT HELPED THEM TO CHANGED. It is the secret to transformation PRAYER !

Let's go, go , go and I will see you at the "TOP" (Transformation Outreach Presidential CLUB) Send me your stories, and testimonies and let's celebrate together!

<u>Welcome to Victory!</u>

My Dear Partners, let us first establish some **vital facts**:

- ✓ God wants the **Best for You**
- ✓ You must **meet God** half way to establish your Blessing
- ✓ You must **not quit** on day 29
- ✓ You must make the 31 days of confessions
- ✓ You will **no longer settle** for seconds
- ✓ You will **gather the best** of the grapes of the land and Eat them
- ✓ You will **be obedient** to God's voice as He establishes himself in you
- ✓ You will hearken, obey and **have strength** in Jehovah Jireh
- ✓ You will prevail against your enemies and **have VICTORY** in JESUS!
- ✓ You will **follow the Path of Your Blessing** all the long days of your life

To establish a thing you must **first decree it**. God has given you the authority to decree a thing with your mouth. That is why it is important to pray out loud. There are however, some qualifying factors to any blessing. You must first "Qualify" to Decree!

Qualifying For Your Blessings

How does one qualify for their blessing? 2 things:

1. You must be Born Again (accepting Jesus as Lord and Savior is a MUST!)

- ☐ You must acknowledge the Power of God through his Son Christ Jesus.
- ☐ You must acknowledge the power of the Holy Spirit singularly, corporately and through the mouth of His Prophet(s).
- ☐ You must believe that the Power of God is activated though agreement (two or more in agreement) with the will of God.
- ☐ You must **NOT** pray against the Word, Will or Essence of God. This would be witchcraft and we cancel its assignment and works of darkness **right now in Jesus Name**.
- ☐ If you do not have a scripture reference for your request, you must seek one and agree with it, to see the power of God manifested in your life.
- ☐ You must be a Tither and an Offering Giver. "To whom much is given, much is required."
- ☐ You must covenant to pray for **Apostle and Bishop Rice as God is leading them in this Prophetic Movement,** and will return to you the prophetic blessing through their prayers.

2. You must Trust God. That this is the Devine Will and Direction for your life. Then you can transform as a vital butterfly in Jesus

<u>Scriptures To Read Each Day</u>

Matt 18:19	Matt 6:9-13
John 16:23	Philippians 4:13-19
John 14:14	Mark 11:23
Isaiah 53:5	Deut 8:1
Psalms 72:19	Deut 1:11
Isaiah 25:1	Gen 12:1-4
Psalm 18:46	Gen 12:7
I John 3:8	I John 13:2
Psalms 3:3	John 14:13-14
Psalms 32:5	Proverbs 18:21
Deuteronomy 28:8	Job 22:27-28
Luke 6:38	Romans 11:26
2 Corinthians 9:8	Acts 2:4
Psalms 1:3	Acts 15:8
Proverbs 10:22	Acts 10:38

God's Answers For Your Questions At Hand

How do I know when I have heard from God?

The will of God can be answered in many ways, however the final word is the WORD of GOD. God will never cross his word. If the scriptures do not agree with something you think you heard in your Spirit, it is not the Spirit of God. Be very sure that God's Spirit is tried and true and will always agree with Him! We cannot pick favorites with people, God is the final answer. If the Word does not agree, then it is not the voice of God. Do not be led by Seducing Spirits or the games of people who would lead you to believe differently. God will not cross his word. After "Rightly Dividing the Word of God," what did His Word say?

What is my Purpose?

Your purpose is to communicate with your father about his will for your life and the lives of those you are responsible for. Doing this will enhance your spiritual growth and direction for you and your divine purpose. Make sure your are communicating with God constantly and continually as he continues to give you his directions .

How does God Really Answer?

God answers vocally, through the reading of his word, through the voice of his Spirit, and through the voice of his prophets. God answers through prayer, praise, worship and prophetic utterances. God is answering through weekly assembly worship and the teaching of your leadership. God rarely answers through people whom are NOT assigned to speak into your spirit. Your answers should come from Godly Appointed Counseling.

What are Gods Answers?

Yes. No. Wait. Yes, but wait. No, this is not my will.

TRANSFORMATION FACTOR PRAYER
For Change and Success

Heavenly Father, we come to you in the name of Jesus, and we receive your quickening in our spirits, hearts, minds, body and soul.

The *quickening of our spirit to manifest your will* in our lives. We bow and worship you, and come to you with praise and thanks giving, in fear and trembling, and in reverence to your desires in our hearts.

You are our Reverend, and no other. *You are the* God that has bestowed great love on us. Therefore we believe that you want us to prosper in every measure of our lives. Father in your Holy Name, the Name of Jehovah, the name of God Almighty, the Name of I am, you are the One and Only True and Living God. As Abraham's seed, *remember us*, according to our tithes and offerings, and the covenant of our fathers who served you as we do. We stand on Deuteronomy 1:11. We receive it in the Spirit of Everlasting Truth.

God *WE now join our faith* with others believing for a turn around, complete and honest in every situation of our lives. Yes, we know you will come through on our behalf. So we confess that your word is over our finances, our heartfelt bounty, our strength, our mental stability, and our cheerful and faithful attitude.

We are *Blessed in the City and Blessed in the Field*. Blessed in all our laying down and rising up. Our day is prepared by you and filled with your glory. Your blessings overtake me in every area of my life. My leaf does not wither, *but brings forth Good and Godly fruit.*

I take authority now in the Name of Jesus over my debt. I speak to you boldly and say be paid off and gone, notes, mortgages, and bills are cancelled and deceased and dissolved. Along with bad relationships and friendships that take my mind off the divine will of God in my life. *I declare my finances flow monthly* in the amount of _____. I redefine my flow so *the water runs towards me* and my needs are met, therefore I know Him as the God of Abundance who richly restores in my life. Abundance is my Grace, and *I walk in the committed authority of My savior Jesus the Christ.* He who pours wisdom, knowledge and understanding on me today.

Therefore I resolve *to restore my faith in my God* through Evangelism, and making soul winning abound towards the Kingdom of God. Father God, I need a turnaround in

_____ , _____,
_____ , and _____
this " Bondage and Oppression" of _____,
_____ , & _____ must cease to exist in my life. Strongman, we bind you away from us, and loose the presence of God to totally captivate us in every area of our mind, will and emotions. Father we receive your directions for this turn around. *Send a word our way by the Prophets of God* to help us in our decisions and spiritual growth.

Now Father we praise you today for this is your day and we put our minds on you to fulfill your promise in us. *We pray for Apostle & Bishop Rice.* Bless them now with Godly wisdom, and send uncommon favor and your protection their way.

Any sins I have committed I repent of them and seek your

forgiveness, as to not block my blessing. Thank you Lord for forgiving me and taking any guilt away from any transgressions. I also forgive any others who have transgressed against me, and that I have transgressed against.

Father, *your Spirit now overflows in me* and in my innermost being. A living water now erupts within me. I praise you for exposing anything to me I need to know, including my enemies and all truth. *I renounce all relationships that dishonor you Lord* and break the power of ungodly soul ties over my mind and emotions. *I proclaim freedom* to be the child of the most high God. Jesus you are my shield and glory. I fear no evil for you are with me, and you are the lifter of my head.   *Therefore my head is filled with praise and glory* as you turn my situation around. Holy Spirit *you are my strength as you turn my life around for the Glory of God.*

Father, *you are my salvation* as you turn my spirit around. You are my Rock as you turn my faith around and towards your purpose for me. You are my life. I live and move in you, because of you and for you, in Jesus Name. I love you Lord, and I receive my turn around. I feel it now, and I know you are in me, and I feel your guidance in me as I become stronger in you.

I will tell others of my victory in you, and *that my life is better* as of you promised it would be. ***Thank You Father for Turning it around for me. TODAY!*** Yes, it is working for my good and turning in my favor!

In Jesus Name, I have the Midas Touch. *Everything I touch turns to Gold.* Souls come to me, money comes to me, and happiness is my friend. I establish the presence of God on the Earth. The wealth of the wicked is mines, and *I am sold out for Jesus! I am a winner* ! In Jesus Name, Amen! Amen! AMEN! *Copyright by Dr JG Rice 5/10/09*

CHAPTER 4

FACING MY PAST

MY NAME IS KELVIN IRVIN. I WAS SPIRITUALLY
LOST AND CONFUSED
I USED THE "IDENTIFYING AND OVERCOMING
RATISM TRANSFORMATION"
TO CHANGE MY LIFE.
HERE IS MY STORY...

KELVIN IRVIN

It all started at 6 and with making choices. I've seen my mom beat, had an experience with my cousin in the bed my boy cousin sexual experience gay experience. I made some choices and while not some good choices, while making em I had to face em, choices don't care how old you are who you are when they arise how you got to face them rather now or later. There just choices and there just made some times you try to run from them but eventually you got to face them, and that's where it all starts for me. Some of them have been hard to face but what do you do but face them, like my Bishop and my Apostle have told me. Man, man up. You got to face them.

So here I am at 32 facing choices I made when I was 6, scary/yeah but hath to be done. I remember playing in the yard with my younger brothers at the age of 6 and a car pulled up and someone in the car saying you wanna go with me and I guess as a lil boy I didn't know no better , mom wasn't home I just looked at the man and just knew something about him, and I said yeah. I jump in the car with him and that's where the roller coaster ride begin.

I've seen all kinds of thing's drugs, beaten of women, jail houses, policies and so on and so forth. You as a lil kid looking at this stuff like it's cool, dad with all different kinds of women, uncle always handing 3. out money and everybody just doing what they wanted to do. I can remember being so young but yet police officers kicking in the door and raiding the housed. Man these things just became the norm. So what do you do but say man when is my turn.

My dad had different plans for me wanted me to play football had me running blocks and but the same blocks he was selling drugs at. I guess you neva know the influence you have on a young kid like myself. I'm looking at my dad looking at everything that's going on. I'm like man bump these blocks, so I remember getting old enough and one of the dudes I knew talked about getting some playas, and I had 40 dollars and I bought 4 of them and I can remember getting them 80 dollars and the power I felt from having that money my own money man what a rush. Hiding from my dad telling people (basa's) of course don't tell my dad cause everybody knew him, but man did this start a revolving door of Juvenile Detention Center after Juvenile Detention Center 4.

I can remember days of crying and crying and lord if you get me out of this one I won't do it again, fighting (break: man it's just amazing recalling) fighting being scared but having to face ground do what you got to do. Man it's crazy I remember my dad coming (visiting Detention Center) and leaving and me crying and crying, and he look at me one time and say ain't no need to cry now you made your bed you got to lay in it, you got to man up, and that stuck with me even through life, you got to man up. So I went through life holding on to things hurts, pains, cuz what you got to man up. So I went through level 8 programs doing time 5. neva thinking I would ever go to prison or anything.

I remember sitting in my level 6 program and an officer from FHP Florida State Penitentiary coming to visit us , talk to us and me saying I aint neva going to prison. Ha. Got out kept doing what I was doing, then county jail felt like well at least I can bail out just craziness, then getting caught up again this time I guess I knew I was gonna get some time. I was tired, tired of the in and out, in and out like this can't be life. I remember a guy walking up to me as I was sitting on the stairs in a jail in Port Saint Lucie. Saying something to me about god and it gave me such a relief I was like yeah, I guess that was the point I surrendered. I was 16. Tired. Went through that just dedicated myself to God. Caught 3 years I've done time here and there but to hear that Judge say 3 years man that broke me down so here we go up the road y.o. Lake Butler got to ride now man that hurt me but had to do it. Bootcamp and everything man this took me for a ride I ain't neva wanna see another jailhouse again this was it for me. End up getting out coming home but wanted to stay away from the old place so I went to live back in ft. Lauderdale where it all began

I ended up getting in the church and staying. Working got married my mom had cancer at the time, mind you I haven't spent my majority of my life with my mom and finally when I say I'm coming home she passing. Married at the time my mom dies a lil while later my wife leaves, left alone, left alone that point it was all about seeking God. People leave ya, but ended up getting married again, experiencing hurts in the church, just life. Going through 7 years of marriage 3 kids unhappy, fornicating, adultery, just going wild still in the church preaching and all. Church finds out I didn't wanna lie I admitted it and so they withdrew from me. I guess it all starts a course of action. I started seeing another female, seeing different things instead of struggling trying to make things work, this women had it going on it was like the good life, big screen TV's and a place to relax just chill, but in the course of this time I fell in love but the old man was still with me in the sense of wow trying to fix things and fix people trying to make things perfect I guess fit me, but it was something about her that just bought a refreshing to me, after all the prostitution and women doing all the wrong things this girl made me love her.

I decided to get married again, but still married to the second wife I had to get a divorce, get the divorce we making plans, I got ideas after ideas. I'm doing music, things look like they are fenna blow up and I'm like dang. Ran into this dude (name anonymous). I remember him telling me things it involved god and with a preaching history/ background I listened, lots of things deep things (least to me) I can remember being in the bathroom cutting my hair and him there with me and him telling me something about the moon and the fake landing the technology then and I just broke down wailing here it is I'm traveling and moving trying to make things happen and this day boom all this happens and it was like dang I was neva the same.

I remember seeing spirits that night. I remember I couldn't be around him it was something just too strong on me a presence I remember feeling suicidal rolling in the bed feeling like I wanted to die feeling lost, I remember the confusion but yet the power like I neva felt before I just wanted more. I didn't understand it but I acted like I did then it came to a point where I just wanted to talk about god. I began to sit with myself talk in my head listen hear God (I guess) I'm smoking drinking doing music didn't want my girl to leave man it was crazy sometimes I didn't feel like myself. Then after all this planning marriage and music ideas I felt like I had to leave like I had to make a choice Stephanie or God, and because I had this love for God I had to make a choice, I made a choice God.

This all leads me to another women house older wiser intelligent had a background or history with these spiritual things, started teaching me stuff and offering me to read books we would talk and talk and I was all over the place, back and forth didn't know what to do I left Stephanie but Stephanie was still with me and here I am with another women. To the point she started to say Kevin can't you see, she/they got something on you and I'm like nawh but still suspicious of the dude. But now I'm looking for answers still seeking God sitting with myself, trying to do business but nothing seems to be working like everything is being blocked then I started to learn about forgiveness all this from things occurring I'm cleaning up the side of road just doing stuff but its teaching me stuff just thinking, thinking, thinking.

I remember releasing to her just feeling like this was the way to my freedom talking releasing and all kinds of stuff began to come up the gay thing from when I was young came up all kind of stuff that I had to face look at myself and say not me. I started thinking even more crazier about gay stuff looking at men different I guess I didn't know who I was no more it affected me so bad me Kevin gay I couldn't accept that mind you we had no sexual intercourse we rubbed penises, but it affected me so bad that I had to face that, why I couldn't look at gay men why I hated them man it was crazy, so with all this going on in me the confusion me looking at men sexually couldn't turn it off although I knew that wasn't me I was losing it, it ran me into my destiny I ended up running into this guy at the bus stop (mind you I ended up getting locked up for a pistol charge in all this) and him giving me a card to this church and I took that card and man it's been the best thing ever happened to me.

I ran into Apostle Rice and Bishop Rice my mother and father, hurt and wounded, confused been poured into with false doctrine but yet they received me with open arms, a lil boy crying out for help, journeying been through so much but finally healing started pouring into me truth, faith and faith things I didn't know before with my history in preaching I began to grow see things differently, love and I didn't know what love was. Yet confused trying to figure things out like a man in a cocoon transforming everyday seeing it more clearer and more clearer. I can even feel the freshness now. After all I been through I never witnessed such a faith and with all my baggage loving me pouring into me and now I see things so differently.

I was reading the other day after Bishop preached a message be ye transformed and not conformed point is transformed changed, just like a man coming through a cocoon one state to another discipleship discipline all those things truly living the Word of God. Choices but direction now. I don't live in fear and when it come up cast it down. Truly transformed. Still faced with decisions now I know The God-Kind Of Life. Thanks to my Apostle Dr. J.G. Rice and Arch Bishop James Rice, I can face my past and am victorious. Stay tuned Dr. J.G. Rice is in the building and world she coming. With a team of Faith walkers supporting her who she have raised poured into as her own. It's on.

To my future wife I love you baby. Truly designed designated for me. Just funny that it's taken me so long to get here, had to take the long way around for God to teach me all the things I needed to know so that I wouldn't make the same mistakes twice or again, my leaders, my leaders, my leaders. Greater Harvest Christian Center Churches Worldwide. Like my Apostle say Birth out by My Leaders, and I'm here to stay mom lets go to the world.

I was just a shell of a man, I once was lost but now I'm fount. I lost a mother but gained a mother I lost or what I looked for in a Dad I got. Neva rejected neva looked down upon and though I'm still learning still discovering me, I'm victorious, what they thought couldn't be done I'm doing through God my leaders conquering every fear overcoming. Like my Apostle told me to say to myself I am an overcomer. My Apostle told me some time ago we gonna write this book and I need you to be able to speak from a point of victory and I can say I speak from a point of victory everything has lead me to my true parents my true destiny what God has plucked out now sending back with NO FEAR!

CHAPTER 5

Overcoming the "Spirit of Jungleism"

Beating the "Spirit of Jungleism"

The negative repetitive behaviors

Many people are in spiritual kindergarten, yes in the spirit. "Kindergarten" of no growth, even though they think they are grown, but they're in kindergarten. They have to be led on every level, like a toddler. You have to keep watch on them because they're so subject to fall to prey to the wrong spirit. So subject to fall to the wrong action and activity. Just so easily led astray. That's why I call it a "Kindergarten Spirit."

I follow what is a simple rule in Greater Harvest Christian Center Churches Worldwide, and that rule is made manifested to keep you out of trouble, and so that you're in contact with your leadership about making decisions that would sometimes railroad you. You may even think "ok that's the right decision to make," but at the end of the day it had the wrong answer and the wrong conclusion. So, we have to lead by Psalms 1, led in the "counsel of Godly, in the counsel of wisdom." Even though we may not like it when the person says "NO" to you, it probably would've helped you out tremendously, to hear no more often. **Most of the time when you get that "No" spoken to you, you really needed it**. The " No" counsel is what we do not want to hear, that's why we fail to go to and ask our leadership for "Godly Counsel" and we prefer to ask our peers, coworkers, and friends. All who do not have the spirit of GODLY counsel of their lives. **The reason we fail to ask our GODLY leadership is that we really do not want the transformation truth.** Really, we already know what they're going to say, and so we want to skip around that truth.

One of the things we use as a measuring stick is basing our lives on the lives of each other, which is probably not a great measuring example. But it surly feels good to our flesh to have someone tell us we're right when we are truly wrong. **Our greatest teacher is to learn to follow your leader and their instructions**. It's just as simple as when you were in school and one of your fellow students told you to do some things, you balanced your response and asked, "Did the teacher tell you to tell me to do that?" It's only a foolish student that is always running off with another student doing stuff they aren't suppose to be doing.

Kindergarteners must prepare themselves to leave kindergartner in 10 short months. So TRANSFORMATION must begin!

Kindergarteners do stuff, and always think they know what they doing. But at the end of the day they'll have on a black shoe, and a blue shoe, a pink sock and a red sock. They'll wear their dress with their shirt inside out. They always have an opinion! **This is how you know you're still in kindergarten, when it has to be your way.** It's not about the greater good of everybody else. Because all kindergarteners say is, "I want...." They're very selfish people.

You can be old and still be a kindergartener. **The fastest way to get out the kindergartener level of spiritual maturity is to do what Jesus says, "seek ye first the kingdom."** Ask yourself, did your actions glorify the kingdom? Is what I'm saying and doing right now giving God glory? Is it about my flesh? Is it about my attitude? Or is it about the kingdom? Or is about me? That's how you know you're growing up. When you can say, "I normally would've done that, but for the sake of the kingdom I'm going to do this. Not that."

Stand up for righteousness!

A lot of times you may have to do that ten or twelve times a day. But it's okay, so that you mature. **Consistency is a factor in transforming.** It is not saying, "I did it yesterday and so I'm not doing it today." Or saying, "I did it this morning but I'm not doing it this evening." Someone said to me (and they thought it was an insult but it's the best compliment that they could have given me), "You want to always be right." Yes, I sure do. I want to be right, and live in righteousness. What do you want, to live life being wrong? You see, you let what people say try to intimidate you and change you from what the word of God says. You have a problem when you're wrong and I have a problem <u>if I'm not right</u>. Because I am supposed to be living righteous, and to live righteously you have to be right.

Learn to stand up for what is right. When people come to you, with the idiosyncrasy and they're comfortable in their level of stupidity, trying to make you feel beneath what you are you can say to them just say, "You know what, you can live that and I will live this. I am not going to be swayed by your belligerent ways or your suppressive thoughts of manipulation that you are trying to put out towards me. **You are trying to make what's good seem bad, and what is bad seem good.**" You must have a defense in place. This is because you must know that this is their level of intelligence over the spiritual things. They are dull.

The Spirit of A PYTHON!

It's like the spirit of a python, all it wants to do is get crawl up on and wrap around you until it continues to suffocate the life out of you with everything and all the energy that it has. Hoping that one day you will take your last breath, then it can squeeze in and devour you. This method of thought is what I call *"Jungleism!"*

Jungleism is all about animal eat animal, plot for plot. It is when we want someone to accept the fact that there's no light at night in your jungle. **It's the Spirit that holds you confined against change and escape towards TRANSFORMATION!** Because your bushes haven't been trimmed back, your trees have not pruned, light cannot get into the places of darkness to give you new growth. Jesus said " I am the light of the world." **When there**

is no Jesus, there is no light! When there is no light, that which is beautiful is so out of control until the atoms and the entire universe cannot penetrate the darkness of the jungle. Even in the mist of the day, in the thick of the bush, those animals that lay dormant under the bushes. They lay for the prey and wait. So that they can eat innocent unknowing "kindergartners." The predators of innocence. They become fat themselves, or they become prey to be eaten by some other species. So goes the repetitious cycle of ignorance. It continues and nothing really lives and everything else is waiting to die.

What's your Jungleism? You're backbiting and suppressive mannerism, you sicken everybody that you come into their presence. Sometimes especially people with intelligence and free from Jungleism that have come out of darkness and they're walking into the light. They are quick to discern and want no part of anything of the jungle. **But to have freedom from jungle is to be freed from the past.**

Often we encounter people that are always bringing up the past. They are the ones always saying, "Oh I remember when you were this… and I remember when you were that… and they said this about you… and they said that about you." They don't even know who you are now, because they never knew who you were then. **They are in the "Cycle of Jungleism."** The same cycle, same path and same tree. They think you're still stuck there. What they saw then was a shadow of who you were to come. But because of the hate and the disrespect in their life, they did not want to take the journey. They truly need a transformation factor. Without transformation they began to be that python, that snake, that monkey, and that rat… to eat your grain and make you feel like God is not with you. I come to tell you today **get out of the jungle,** and let the jungle get out of you. Get out the jungle! Come out of the jungle!

The jungle, in my definition to make this point, is that thing that's going to keep you from where God intended for you to be. It's the bushes, it's the vines, it's the darkness, and it's the repetitious stupidity that causes us not to TRANSFORM into greatness and bring GLORY to our Creator.

We teach our men to dress like men, because that is supposed to make you look presentable. You can control the elements of your life, that's going to lead you to your future. But when you're stuck in the jungle you run around like a "pigmy." You run around like you are "Tarzan looking for Jane." Speaking in undeterminable words because you're speaking to animals that are not even on your level. You are thinking that you're controlling something, while really you are being controlled. Never being set free, until you set your own mind free. You must be transformed out of "Jungleism."

Using the **58 Transformation Factors to Success**, that God has taught me, and allowed me to teach others will set you free!

Using the power of **Godly Communication** to help TRANSFORM your life.

When you fail to communicate properly, you are operating in "MONKEYISM"

We call it "Monkeyism" because we have not learned to declare and decree a thing. We are so intelligent yet we don't free ourselves to live limitless in God. Are you still in the jungle? You might as well be an ape or a monkey by the way you treat yourself and the way you've been treating others. The way you communicate is unreal to the kingdom. Verbal abilities with you power.

Many times we have no vision. An ape and a monkey has no vision, other than swinging from tree to tree. Their vision is limited by their environment. A lion has vision, they go from territory to territory. They began to circle in places and call themselves family. An elephant has a vision, whales have vision, and salmons have visions. **A restrained person has no vision, the only vision you have is a "television."** That's why somebody else's vision is telling you what to do. God told me, "there are test in your life that you must past if you intend to truly come into the land, the knowledge, and the lifestyle of ZOE! You have to come out of the dumb dumb, come through church dumb, and come into the kingdom."

That's the problem. Many of us do not want to become kingdom minded. In this season of your life, review your associates and make up in your mind, **"I don't want anybody that's not kingdom minded around me because you drain too much energy from my present and my future."** So you have to be willing to tell your mother, your brothers, your sisters and whoever, "If you must act like a failure, do it somewhere else because I don't intend for you to python me."

You can go to certain neighborhoods and the grass won't grow because of the residents that live in the neighborhood. **Some people don't have the spirit of progress in their life. They kill everything.** They do not having enough sense to water the grass. They think the grass is made to put broken down cars on. A kingdom minded person will take a broken car that they do not intend to fix and sell it to a broken minded person. A broken minded person will not even have enough sense to sell the car to make more money. The scriptures tell us to " buy, sell, trade and gain more." But they'll entertain the roaches and the rats with tea parties and cookie (meaning shopping till they really drop). They'll have several hundreds of dollars per month, and are broke from month to month, living paycheck to paycheck. "Monkeyism" is all about, "What can you do for me? What you can do for me? It's all about me, me, me and my tree!"

When will you come out of the Monkeyism test? When are you going to past the test? You have to learn it's not about you, it's about the kingdom. When is your light bulb going to come on? When will you realize that God has an assignment and a purpose for you? When is your ding ding ding ding bell going to finally be answered? That it's not about you, it's about the kingdom! **Only what you do for Christ will last.**

The Jungleism of Relationship

Don't let anybody play with your mind. Women must become smarter, not so needy or lonely. Going along with anything just to have someone to call, talk to on the phone, to lie to you by filling you up with craziness and stupidity (which you already knew they were not going to do anything they said). **So who's the joke really on?** You call yourself a Mack daddy, or somebody, and the time and energy you spend on being "so manipulative" you could have spent on kingdom assignment. So who won? The jungle won.

What are you offering?

What are you offering now that you're out the jungle? What are you bringing to the table? You came out the jungle, but you're still acting like a monkey. We must be able to plant our feet and rise up, and be the man of God that God has called you to be. The woman of God that God has called you to be. The people of Transformation unto Godliness and holiness A people of praise and power, a people of Victory! We must become stable in God. **We cannot be like a monkey, jumping and running from our trials and tests.** Every time you don't like a tree, you jump from that tree to the next. That sounds like a monkey to me. Swinging around care free.

Others of us have the opposite actions of **the "Do Nothing" spirit**. We are still acting like a lion, sitting around and waiting on the females to go to work every day to bring you back everything you need. "You have to eat first," that sounds like the jungle to me. Others have **the "Swamp Creature" spirit**. You're still acting like an alligator swimming around seeing who you're going devour. Who's going to be stupid enough to fall for one of your tricks. So when they put their foot in the water and thinking it's all clear, up pop the alligator. The transition has to happen now! The transformation factor has to take place now!

What's in you? What's in you? Are you the Owl of the Jungle? The sounds of the jungle that won't let you rest at night? So you can't go to sleep like somebody with a vision and a purpose. Do you stay up all night just scheming? Only watched by the owls that disappear in the day time waiting for the night to come. Watching and becoming wise to the ills of those that lurk in the mist of the darkness. We must transform from all "JUNGLEISM" and today is a great day to start.

Playing lizard games! A "Geico Spirit"

"I thought he was going to be different." Why? You didn't know him but for two weeks and got him in your bed and trying to move him into your house. Why did you think it was going to be different? You didn't even know him. You didn't even know her. You didn't even know her baby daddy was a foolish hot head, but you see five babies and no daddy. We are so "deep and wonderful." You have it all together, but really what you have is a "Jungle Mentality." An eat it up mentality.

So we must not think we're winning the race by involving somebody else in our Jungleism, our Monkeyism and our Ratism. When all I'm doing is killing myself. Why? Because the jungle ages you so quickly, that's why people that live that kind of life look so old and raggedy and beat up. They die before their time. That's why they never really gain anything to show for the life they have led, because they never really changed their mind set. So you can come out the Jungle but can the Jungle really come out of you?

Doesn't this sound like Israel with that Egyptian mentality? Yes it does! Will you create another jungle where you are now? Deep within yourself, will you just create another Jungle? Will you invite those animals back into your jungle because you really don't want to let go of what you came out of? Change is a powerful word. **If you come to change than there should be some signs.** Lots of change brings Victory. You have to let it go so that God can come in, and the light can come in and shine in the mist of darkness. Because where there is light there is no darkness. Cut the bushes down so light came come in. The scriptures say, "the light comes, and the darkness doesn't even understand it, the darkness comprehends it not!" I'm glad to be light. Someone must be the light.

A Garden–vs-A Jungle

I don't want a Jungle, I just want a Garden. There's a difference in a garden and a jungle. We have to change ourselves. Stop fooling yourself and change, least you get older and still keep the same old ways. **There will always be others in the jungle younger than you that do the things that you thought you could do.** They will move you out the way, trying to displace you. In the Jungle you always fight for rank, love, space, and food because that's the life of the jungle. That's what Scar was about, (Uh, did you miss the whole message of the Lion King?) taking over. That's why even in a gang there's always someone looking behind you and looking over your shoulder. You have to look to see who really wants to see you fall and who is trying to take you over. Who's that new person that's rising up to replace me? In Christ you transition into interdependency, glad for extra help. **We should be happy to grow, not devour each other.** That's transformation. Why wouldn't you want to live like that? Personally, I'm irreplaceable, but I am not in the jungle.

"I come to the garden alone while the dew is still on the rose, and the joy that I hear as I tarry there, none other have ever known. For He walks with me and He talks with me and He tells me that I am His own and the joys we share as we tarry there none other have ever known. The secret places of the most high is where I abide. We shall abide under the shadow of the All Mighty. I will say to the Lord, He is my refuge, my fortress in whom I trust. Because he have never seen the righteous (the one that wants to be right) forsaken nor the seed of the righteous begging bread".

There are certain anointing even on my children, because they are the seed of the righteous. There are certain anointing on this house because you're a seed of the righteous. That's why it's good to know somebody is saved in your family. So you can claim that inheritance. So I can say, "That's mine!" But you must have a change of mind. Where ever you are I've just identified you because **if you aren't a son or a daughter of God, than you are a "man or a babe" of the world**. But you change your mind! If we are to transform we must get our mind right!

Watch what you touch in the jungle it will KILL YOU!

There are certain flowers that you don't touch in the jungle. Plants that will kill you instantly. That goes to show you that everything silver isn't gold, and everything shiny isn't silver. You go to touch some of those plants and you'll never make it out alive. Beautiful they are, but very dangerous. That's true in life as well.

Don't involve yourself in everything that looks good, it may kill you or make you very sickly. When we transform, we learn our environment. What is a blessing and what is a curse. We were created to be a blessing, not a mess! God wants us to transform to his image. Not a image of negative thoughts, complainers, mummers, or doubters. Let's begin to change, to be the blessing God created us to be. Some people look beautiful but they are poisonous. But you'll never know just how contaminated they are until you touch them. Beautiful like a Venus Fly Trap. Remember that show "Little House of Horrors" and the that plant that was eating people? It got just a touch of blood. Some people are fly traps. Some people look like little fishes but they are really piranhas. Some of you are piranhas. You look so innocent. But if you put someone with you, then the jungle in you will come out.

I was a hot and a cold mess. Yes, even I was garbage before God saved me. That's why our ministry is based on you transforming. It's a major part of my ministry. To identify those caught in the FLY trap and try to free them before they are consumed. I believe I am even doing it now. Called to rescue the young people, because God rescued me young. There is a message of Hope by my life's testimony. You can make it through it ALL, and be it All in Christ Jesus. There is no failure. **God saved me young, and kept me in his Holy Ghost power**. What He has done for me He can still do for you. Jesus is the Answer, and I do not have another answer! That's my story, praising my Savior, all the daylong! Yes, I was a monkey in the jungle, a rat, and a python. I needed a savior. I was a mess! I had been there and done all that, and was on my way to a burning hell on a 747 with a beef stick and I didn't even know how to smoke it. I just had to have one, because everybody else had one. Just hold it like it's cool, I was a big dummy. And God snatched me out, **YOUNG**, and rescued me. Saved me. He took that jungle out of me. He took it out so much so that my "so called family" despised me (because I was not longer in the jungle with them). They never talked about me when I was a sinner. But when I gave my heart to Jesus, they had so much to say. I recognize now that nobody wanted to see me leave the jungle, especially if they were left behind.

I'd rather be kept in a zoo then out in the wild.

Do you know that the others are mad, because now they're sitting on the big rock's chilling. There's nobody fighting to get bananas every day, living like kings and queens. They don't even have to find the water to give them a bath in there, the water never runs dry. Some people get rescued and get mad about not being in the jungle anymore. These people really do try to leave the safety too. Not me. I am just fine right here, nice and kept, right nice and cool. "Metro Zoo" me, because at least that's better than being in the wild.

They pick a certain kind of animal to go to metro zoo. If you come in there trying to act all aggressive, trying to fight, beating down on everybody, acting a fool and with bad diseases, they will put you to sleep because you are upsetting the environment. **When God pulls us out, how can we not be grateful?** He puts us in the kingdom "metro zoo" and takes care of the environment. He feeds us, take care of us, he want let the rain hit us to bad, he controls the climate, and he keeps it at the perfect temperature just for us. God takes care of us, and we can be so ungrateful. The animals are treated well. Like the Seal, all he has to do is clap and here comes the zookeeper to give him some food. Just do what you do naturally. God is not telling you that you can't be a seal any more. He's just telling you that the environment that you were in was to toxic and dangerous for you. So He places you in a new environment so He can take care of you. WOW! What a God and a great Savior we have.

So now we are in the company of some good Kangaroos to hang out with. Some good Hippopotamus to hang out with. You know who those good animals are. The big shots of the zoo, and it doesn't have anything to do with size, its attitude. I'm talking about the ones with a big attitude. That "Hippo Mentality." All a hippo really does is just stand there and do nothing. God has a place for all of us, and purpose for all of us.

Passing the Grateful Test on our way to TRANSFORMATION

There are some test you have to pass in order to grow up. One thing is to begin to become grateful. Are you grateful? Do you know how to really be grateful? If you only have a piece of bread, be grateful. If you have peanut butter to put on the bread, be grateful. If you have a little jelly to add with it, be grateful. If you have a slice of bologna, be grateful. If you have the bologna and no bread, roll it up and eat it slow. Make a party and eat it with a toothpick and just be grateful. Because God chose you. He chose you! **You are His "chosen people," a peculiar nation.**

When we are grateful we stop trying to contaminate other people's environment with foolishness. We learn to stay in our cage and NOT to be the "JONES." Stay in your cage, because if you get in the wrong cage with the wrong folks that have true animal instinct, those instincts are going to come out. Go ahead and be the little rabbit hopping on over to the Mr. Lions cage. You know Mr. Rabbit will not have anything but fur in the air. Then Mr. Rabbit's family at the funeral will say, " I thought they were friends?"

That's why you don't get along with certain people. **Certain species just don't run together. Either you're going to eat them or they're going to eat you.** So you have to know what's in somebody's nature. You have to know what's in their nature, and expect them to be who they are even in the zoo. Zoo Keepers (pastors) are very IMPORTANT because we keep the links together and yet separate. Zoo Keepers and Kingdom Keepers keep the Lions over here and the Bears over there. I say Kingdom, but some of us are still in the zoo. We keep the birds over here and the snakes over there. When we put all the animals in one place, from one species to another, everybody will have a nice time at the zoo. We're still at the zoo, ok ... "the Kingdom, they're still in the kingdom."

Let's have a reality check as we laugh about life. The truth is everybody is not fit to be in the cage with everybody, and it's the zookeepers responsibility to make sure that the people of like minds and spirits stay in their designed cages. That way everybody can enjoy the view (the worship service). So when people pay to get into the zoo, everything looks beautiful and organized. So is such in the kingdom. **When we come into the Kingdom everything is organized, everything has a place and a purpose**. Everybody has a place and a purpose. Please find your place and bring forth fruit.

You are reproducing who you are!

Monkeys need to expect to have monkey babies, not baby zebras and crocodiles. Sometimes we wonder why our witnessing does not affect certain people. It's because they don't have your spirit. You're not going to reproduce anything but your own kind. "Bring forth fruit, after your own KIND and your fruit shall remain."

That's why you can meet those five to ten people in your life and it felt like you've known them forever. It's because they're of your species and more than likely you all enjoy the same things. You all want to go to the same places. Not because trouble or tainted pasts bringing you together, because your past does not always determine your future. It was like that when Bishop Rice and I met, **we knew we were supposed to be kingdom keepers together.**

These people become your friends and that friendship remains. It doesn't matter what storm happens, you will always be FRIENDS. These are the kinds of friends that you may not even talk to each and every day. Those kind of true friends you don't have to talk to everyday. But when you talk to them it's like BAM! Nothing has changed and the conversation just flows. Those are the person's you call **long term friends**.

I'm talking about true friends I am not just talking about knowing someone for 20 minutes . NO, I mean true friends that have been through something with you. We've had an argument, we all most fought, and we're still together. That's friendship! But if your friendship can't take any cross words from time to time, then that's not a "friend", that's probably just an associate. These friends sharpen you and push you to a greater destiny and a life of success. They help you transform into a greater person. These are keepers. On the other hand there are friends who bring out the worse in you. These may be people to eliminate from your transformed life.

I have two people in our ministry that are 35 year friends. They are the best of "arguing friends" I ever seen in my life. They argue at least five times a month. I believe that's their medicine for each other, but they have been there for each other through thick and thin. They can only talk about the bad things that have happened to each other. Is this a good healthy relationship? No, of course not, and they probably will do better apart. But yet they hang in there. **I want true good friends, and to get this you have to be a friend.** Some of us can't keep good people in our lives for two days. However Bishop Rice and myself have had friends that we have had for years in our life, and they are saved and POSITIVE people. They are ever growing, and this keeps us growing as well. No we do not always agree, and we might not believe in all the same things. Like if it will rain today or not! But we maintain the same core values. **Agreement is important, two can only walk together if they agree**. One thing about it, we believe Jesus is Lord, and they know if God tells me something I'm going to tell them. And I respect that same anointing in their life. Iron does sharpen iron. So I'm not looking for the difference in people, I am looking for what do we have in common? That's how we're going to determine if we can walk together, because to be vital to one another we must have agreement. So find out in your life cycle of connections, what do we agree on and build on that.

To have positive relationships we must start focusing in our mind, "What do we agree on?" And that should be the question that will cause our friendship, relationship, family unit and even our church family unit to stand and be strong. "What do we agree on," is a strong and powerful question. You may find that you have more that you agree on, then what you don't agree on. That's when you're on the road to something powerful! **This is called the factor of multiplication.** You will not just add to your being, you will begin to multiply!

Transformation Causes Multiplication!

When you operate in positive agreement you can multiply visions, and multiply dreams You will begin to multiplying stuff, because stuff comes to people that agree with each other. What we agree on is **VITAL** . This is what you have to base your life on. If you are with somebody you can't agree on with anything, that is NOT your person to transform with. If you have to explain everything and always defend yourself, that's not the person to transform with. There are one of four things happening in this relationship:

1) Either they are your coach/pastor/ leader/ supervisor and you are supposed to take instructions from them, and you

are being rebellious.

2) They are your" true" friend trying to help you see our ways of folly and you are in denial.

3) They are Your Teacher, spouse or instructor in growth and development, and you don't want to grow up. Or…

4) They are someone God has sent to help you to grow up into Godly behavior, and you DO NOT WANT to receive their help, or you think they are in your way, and you are right and they are wrong.

Either way there needs to be a breaking and blending of the minds to transform and come into agreement with each other Or at some point you must just agree to depart and find others paths to success .This relationship will be to stressful for each of you until someone TRANSFORMS!

I'm talking about your circle of friends. I'm not speaking about your leaders. The leader is here to lead you and you're here to "swallow and follow". This comparison test is for you to learn to take instructions and not to try to TRANSFORM your leader into complying with your downwards spiral, but to receive a hand up of instructions, and power from your set man or woman of faith.

Don't Be DUMMIFIED, Transform your MIND TODAY!

Dummified is when you know you're making **DUMB** mistakes and refuse to acknowledge them, or change from doing them over and over again. **Only you know your level of stupidity that you have been living and doing all of your life.** I only know my level of Godliness that I've been living. So when someone comes up to you to impress upon you, their level of ignorance to change you or to make you react to an action that will bring you into a zone where you're really not comfortable. Then you have to

85

recognize that's the trick of the devil, to make you fail that particular test in your life.

The Life Test
You will have to pass it to become TRANSFORMED.

The life test is surrounded by standards and challenges that are meant to be conquered to transform. Challenges that make you say, "This is my standard, based on the word of God." Because if it is not based on the word of God, then it has no standard. It's just a bunch of crap. We must learn to say, "This is my standard and this is my scripture so I can stand on the word of God. I am not here in this level of life to stay. I am going forward. **I must learn that the Seat I am in today is not the final Seat of my LIFE.** I must move life Seats to get to where I need to go. I will not be sitting in this kindergartner chair in 10 years. The chair will be too small for me. And so to TRANSFORM I must be comfortable with my move of seats." That what you do when you actually come to one classroom, and stay in that class, until you're promoted to another class. You then have to move seats. You are no longer in 1st grade, stop going to that class, you just moved Seats. You should accept the fact that you should be promoted and expect to see yourself to another seat.

How do I get to another seat where I'm not acting defeated? Where I don't need the spot light and really don't need the attention of negativity? When you create and surround yourself with so much negative energy, sometimes you are not allowed to pass to the next level because you did not learn your materials in the grade you were in. You were "Held Back." The bottom line then is that it's really the person, the student, that needs to fix the problem (and needs their heart fix) and needs an attitude check. But instead of taking that mirror of life and saying, "You know what, that's me. I was the problem over there. I was the problem right there. Then I got over here and I was the problem here as well." **So I Failed. I didn't get promoted. I did not pass the test."** Even though I tried to manipulate the mind sets of others that were weak and tried to blame the teacher. To make the Church think that they were the problem. Then somebody rose up and told me, "No! You're the problem." But you didn't want to receive that, and now you come back full circle and you are back to having to past the test of life. **This time Do the Work, pass the grade, pass the test and get promoted.** TRANSFORM and go higher to another seat!

You must recognize what you did wrong, to do it right next time!

To past the test means you have to recognize what you did prior in your life to make you not pass the test? If you were looking for a 100, but you made a 20, then you were way off. **But if you were looking for a 100 and made an 89, then you have a few things to correct to get that passing score!** So then you have to assess how you did on the things that brought you to this level. The things that I will pass or fail in this particular circumstances. Did I do better than what I would've done and run as far as I did had I not had the information that I had? Or did I really do a whole lot better than I would've done last year this time?

Challenges will come, hurdles are made to be jumped.

They made hurdles and then they made horses jump them. They made hurdles and then they asked people to leap over them. **A hurdle is not necessarily there to stop you.** But if you can't jump it, then why don't you just walk up to it and kick it down. Step over it and keep going. But you have to be able to finish this course. Fight a good fight. Keep the faith. Finish the course. Graduate and keep going. Life has too much to offer to stop there!

"So how do I finish the course Apostle?" I'm so glad you ask me, because I want to tell you just that. You have to begin to decree and declare. Stop talking about what you were or are not. Stop being so negative and rehearsing the past mistakes. **A lot of defeats come when you spend time on all the wrong things.** I rarely speak of negative things in my life. I have too much good that God has done for me and with me to focus on the bad. The first time somebody meets you, all you want to do is tell them about is all the dirt in your past because you can't see the light in your future.

When all you can do is talk about the dirt in your past it's because you are a limited minded person. If you all you can do is talk about what somebody did 20 years ago, than really you have no life. You do not need to hold on to that place in life that you thought was your **BAD PLACE**. The place that you was less than what they should have been. Please don't live your life in a memory so bad that you can regurgitate it over, to keep yourself in a non-productive state. **JUST LET IT GO, DIE and stop visiting the grave site!** It really is over! This has been designed as a negative behavior by the enemy of your destiny to make yourself feel better about yourself. Even forgive others FAST and move on to another seat. So when that person pops up again, you are not where they left you because you have passed your test!

Bitterness is a Python Spirit

Do not become negative and bitter and your conversation reflects that's your attitude. The way you look and the disposition you give off. Becoming negative is past "Snakeism." It's just as the spirit of a Python. All it wants to do is get crawl up on you, get around you until it continues to suffocate the life out of you with everything and all the energy it has. Hoping that one day you'll take your last breath, and the Python will squeeze that final squeeze and you'll breathe no more. The very life and cycle of the Jungle.

That's JUNGLEISM

The fastest way to get out of kindergarten, the kindergarten level of spiritual maturity, is to do what Jesus says, "Seek ye First the Kingdom of God." Don't focus on what you want, focus on the needs of your Leader and pray for their needs. When you do this for 30 days God will begin to turn your life around. Pray about it and then leave it at the altar, then get busy doing what the Lord told you to do. Then you'll past the self-test and get promoted to the next level. Pray about it and then leave it there, and do what God told you to do. Start by learning what your assignment is. That's why God took you through that metaphoric journey, to understand who you are not so you can see who you ARE. **You can't do Gods will if you don't know God's will.**

Jungleism in Relationships

Gods will is not for you to find out how many women or men you can get on a "string," that's Satan, that's the devil. And what does he want to do? He wants to dis-image the image that God has said that two will become one flesh and become married. Because "marriage is honorable and the bed is undefiled." Anything else, you're a whoremonger, a fornicator or an adulterous and you'll have no place in the kingdom. "What are you saying Apostle?" I'm saying that **in the Jungle we cohabitate and mate with anything moving that's hot.** Anything that displays itself in a provocative manner and says, "Here I am, come and copulate. But I'm not going to be there with you for life, and I will not help you raise anybody or anything. I'm just going to hit it and quit it and go to somebody else." That's in the jungle. Now you are left to fend and tend for those that you birth, against all the elements of those things that tried to take you out.

The truth is the Jungle is all about survival of the fittest. You may just happen to make it or not, if you are fit enough! And now you have three or four little ones that you are trying to raise in a manner without that person being there that was so "hot for you" just nine months ago. You were in a Jungle Life, not Jungle wife! Just a year ago they told you everything you wanted to hear, you heard the **ROAR of the JUNGLE.** Now they are no longer in the picture, but the copulation is complete and the Jungle has swallowed them and you up again. Like the Lion... You are like the wolf... You are like the hyena... You are like the Bear.. taking care of your cubs in the jungle of LIFE.

It doesn't impress me for a man to tell me how many children he may have, tell me how many are you taking care of. Or for a woman in that fact. You can't be saved say that you can't take care of your kids. Something is wrong with your Holy Ghost. I don't care who you are, if you can't send that child support check buddy you are not saved. If you can't buy pampers something is wrong. You are still Jungle Minded. When they are grown they, like all Eagles, fly for themselves. But while they are cubs, take care of them. This Transformation must happen for society to function in a healthy environment.

We gather those around us that make us feel good about who we are. We get other boys to hang out with us under the "tree" to tell all our lies to, because they can tell lies themselves. We go to the beauty shop ladies and tell our lies. "Child I got him wrapped around my finger...," but then go home and cry. Because not only did you have him but Susie, Marsha and Tonesha had him too. Betty Wright told the story, **"The truth is nobody has him because he does not even have his self."** He is just a broke down old Lion, put out of the pride and replaced by Simba. Wandering around trying to find somebody. Just a little boy trying to get a bottle. He may have the term of "man" behind his name because the number signifies getting older, but I really didn't change.

Jungleism in the Church

And then you come into the church and bring the Jungle in the church. Many people are really not getting saved anymore. Bishop and I watch the cycle of defeat coming into the church. We see church going girls meet a guy and their salvation goes out the window. Let me show you the cycle… You have somebody, you don't even know, kissing on you within 24 hours of meeting them because you're just that desperate. Because you're in the jungle. How did you meet? You visited the Jungle Chat Rooms and Online Dating sites. You went to a club with the tightest clothing that you can possibly wear then come to church with the same attire. **You put on a show with your provocativeness and nakedness to seduce someone that you think you're really winning.** Then that person turns up with HIV and pumps you up with a baby that has HIV and nobody even knows his name. Now who has to comfort you? **THE CHURCH!** This forest of belief is held all in the name of L-O-V-E. All in the name of love.

No one can love you if they don't love themselves. If they can't respect themselves, they can't love themselves. So you play the same games over and over, affecting your life, your children's lives, and the people that really love you always get caught up in the middle of the Jungle with you and your cubs. I hope this causes some young mother on child number 3, working on child number 4 or 5, to stop and say, "This behavior must change for my life to change. I am doing nothing with my body but breaking down my life, my health and my mind. **TODAY I will begin a TRANSFORMATION FACTOR!**"

Jesus operated this way. What way? Seeking first the kingdom. "I didn't come to do my will, I came to do the will of who?" The father! He was not self-focus, he did not operate in self-interest, and he always had the plan of God on his mind. When you speak with someone and you ask them, "What is your future plan?," and it doesn't include God...drop that zero. Because you don't have a hero, male or female. If their plan doesn't include the plan of God, and they are of age, you don't have anyone **SPECIAL**. You only have someone that wants to **TRAP** you like they're trapped in the jungle. You don't even have a good friend.

How am I to become a blessing to my life and the people in my life? You have to pass your test. Stop acting. Let's talk about a show called "Gilligan's Island." On Gilligan's Island, there was this fancy boat that got ship wrecked on a deserted island for some fifty years (well to me it looked like fifty because nobody grew old). Every time they would get something done right (you know to get off the island), somebody would end up doing something stupid and they would have to wait another time around until another ship came by. **You don't have to be like the castaways of Gilligan's Island**, you can say to yourself, "I am getting out of this Jungleism Mentality. I am getting off this island. I will not be like Gilligan. You will not make a show about me." And Mrs. Howell with her fancy clothes and big money, and can't spend a dime because she's trapped on the island. You are trapped on the island in your mind. I just think I would've got together with those people and build me a boat or at least went to another island. Build a boat, build a float, anything, but let's do something! Just don't stay here. Let's get out of the JUNGLE!

Don't be selfish! Don't be self-centered!

Don't be like Gilligan, stuck on the island. You can do something with yourself. Jesus operated this way. He was not self-focus. Ask yourself this question, "Are you all about yourself?" Because if you are, you're going to be by yourself. The reality is that people might be around you, but they are not going to with you. You are going to find out sooner or later that everybody is going to start kicking you out of their lives because they recognize that you are all about yourself. **Positive people are learning how**

to disconnect from negative forces of energy! They are secure enough to tell you "to take yourself, and go with yourself, by yourself " and still love Jesus. The sad news is, when you get with the next person and they find out who you really are, then they are going to kick you out as well. If you don't come out of your mental Jungle, you are going to find out that every time you have to get kicked out you lose something. So only being about "self-interest" is not a good thing.

Being selfish is not a good thing. Being all about you isn't a good thing. You need to work with the program. He, Jesus our Lord and Savior, always had a plan of God on His mind. The plan was to minister to other people. For He said, *"I came down from heaven not to do my own will, but to do the will of him that sent me." (John 6:28)* So based on that, **YOU didn't choose God to bring you out of the jungle, GOD chose to bring you out.** God reached down and pulled you out. Like a recue on lost and found. Some people may not get pulled out and many will be left behind. Left behind in the jungle. Left behind in life. But He pulled you.

Now that your recognize that God has had favor on you and your life, let's use the 89 Transformation Points of Success to help you transform and stay out of the Jungle. As I said earlier, "this is also my testimony." God had to take me out of the jungle in many areas, but I was willing to go. And **I hope by being transparent, it will help you to know you too can leave the Jungle for the Garden.**

There is an old hymn that says, "I come to the garden alone, while the dew is still on the rose, and the voice I hear calls me every clear, but the Sound of Christ atonement. And He walks with me, and He talks with me, and He tells me I am his own. And the Joy we share as we tarry there, no other has ever known." Again I encourage you to leave and come to God's blessed Garden. There in prayer you will find strength, love, peace, happiness, temperance, faith, meekness, kindness, and so much more…

It is our prayer that the favor of Christ will meet your every need as you transform using these last precious keys that will cause you to succeed.

CHAPTER 6

FROM NOBODY TO SOMEBODY

MY NAME IS MARIAH MASON. I WAS TORN UP FROM THE FLOOR UP! I USED THE "IDENTIFYING AND OVERCOMING THE SPIRIT OF JUNGELISM" TO CHANGE MY LIFE. HERE IS MY STORY...

MARIAH MASON-THOMPSON

I step out the car and call her, Jazz was a Indian Elderly Woman who work at my job, When Jazz pick up I ask her did she loose her wedding rings, She Replied," YES YES WHERE ARE THEY" I told her that I had them, and that she had left it in the restroom, I told her that the Lord had just spoke to me and told me that the rings was hers. I ask Jazz where she was so I can drop off the rings. I went back to tell Sherry that I had to go somewhere so she stay at the Girl house. While I left I didn't tell what had happen or what I was doing, As I was driving crying and giving thanking God The lord begin to show me myself that he was getting ready to change my life, He also showed me a man kneeling down putting a ring on my finger.

I arrive to Jazz house and returned her rings back to her, As I was in her house I ask Jazz if she believe me, I wanted to make sure it was unbelievable to me I must be honest I couldn't believe it.. Jazz yes I believe I have a relationship with God, Jazz was thanking me I gave her hug and went back where Sherry was, All Night I kept thinking about what had happen I was uncomfortable I was so guilty before God I had just kiss a girl and was on a pill, I sat down the whole time and the club with Sherry asking me why you not dancing what's wrong with you, I kept saying I'm alright my feet just hurting I was lying. I just couldn't say what happen I couldn't wait to get home,

When I got home I kept Repenting and asking God to help me, I thought on it for about a week. One-day while sitting in my living I ripped up my blunt and said I'm not gone smoke no-more Marijuana,
Couple weeks after that I fought my cousin wife for running over my niece, His wife was also pregnant and I got arrest for 2nd degree Felony battery on a pregnant woman. My first time going to a County Jail, I cried like a baby in the sell I had all kind of thoughts running cross my head that made me keep crying, I was a lot of over thinking, I call my family asking them to bond me out

everybody said they don't have no money and they was the one who let her call the police on me put was trying to save her from going to jail running the baby before I fought her, Finally my Dad sister found a Lady who said she come get me for free since I had a Job I would just have to pay her back, I was excited I said GOD is Awesome, They released me I paid the bails-bonds man but I couldn't pay my rent, I had waited too late to ask the Landlord can I have some-time to pay the rent I was in the process of being evicted, I had to move back in with my Grand-mother.

I lost my car while staying with my grandmother I went to my Dad church that he used to take me to in Pompano, Florida. I had $20 dollars on me I said I'm going to put this and church I was expecting something God ,And what I got from Church was the Man Of God said pray for God to send you Leader after His Heart, I went back to my Grandmother and I prayed for God to send me a Leader after his heart. I took a nap then got up to take my sister to work and we put the kids and the I got on I-95 South to take her to work. All of A sudden my hood flew up and hit the front window by the Grace of God I was able to control the car, And no glass shatter in our face, The hood was bent and the front window was crack bad.

My aunt came and brought a rope to tie down hood so I can drive the car back home. I found A flyer that buy Junk cars and I sold my car to them. God knew what he was doing I was already driving with suspended license and out on bond. Two weeks after losing my car I went to the store down the street from my grandmother house I was back praying and talking to God. Then my phone start ringing I answer the phone I receive a call from Arch Bishop James Rice I was getting ready hang I thought he was somebody out of town, I didn't hang because everything he was saying was like for me. Then the phone said to leave a message press 1 so I did and I told everything I was going through and everything I was doing.

The next day Bishop call me and I spoke with him personally I was confessing my smoking habits ,and everything I was going through. He prayed for me invited me to church, He also said that he do counseling session and I agreed to take counsel, I knew I needed it I felt like my change was coming He told me he wife was gone be preaching and that she was anointed. I was excited I couldn't wait to come. I went back to the store got me a money order and mail it off for my counseling section. That Friday came when I got off of work I went straight to Greater Harvest Christian Center. This was almost the end of the month of April 2012 when I receive a call from Bishop and I step foot in Greater Harvest.

When I step foot inside the Harvest there was something that felt so different about it, I felt the Power Of God in the House. Everybody was praising God on One-A-Cord and I was praising God not being ashamed I didn't have nobody looking at me crazy I recognize that I was in a house that praise God.

The Woman Of God came up, as she was walking the floor preaching the word of God my eyes was glued to her, I loved what I saw, a woman that stand so boldly for God, speaks the truth, and speaks what thus say the LORD. It was my first time being in there while she was preaching the word so good nothing but true, that word was for me it was like I was there on the right time. I would "YES LORD, AMEN, PREACH" I never said nothing in church when the pastor will preach I was afraid to open mouth, I knew people would stare at you. There something different about the Harvest. Chief Apostle Dr. J G Rice pointed at me and told me to come to her she spoke in my life, And everything she spoke was true. I remember as she was speaking she told me God is changing your life and He gone allow you to tell your Testimony. She had also prayed over some oil which was call BUST IT.

She told me to get 21days of Prayer, a CD that she was releasing that night. I came I knew I needed both of them, After service I had my sister to bring me all my money from selling my car and I got both.
After leaving from service my sister ask me do I want to hit the cigarette, I replied No I'm not smoking them no more I had just got a word from the Lord seen how the house of God was on Fire that Night I had got my Oil and Cd's I wasn't going for that, I ready to come back on Sunday.

I work Sunday's on my job at 5am till 11am I will rush out the Job and come straight to the Harvest I knew that Harvest for me I tried figuring out how my number got on the call list, I couldn't all knew was it was nobody but God I had to keep coming It was time to Change I couldn't wait to hear Apostle preach. I inspire the way she live for God and Not Afraid to speak what God say, How she not moved by people feelings, has no Fear, Most of The Love she Share.

One-day before I was going to Church I was thinking in maybe I'm too young to live for God, I came to church that night and Apostle prophesied to me and said don't worry about how young you is to serve, she said God saved me when I was the same age as you, I was thinking how she knew that I just was thinking about that earlier.
I said that's a true Prophet. After that I made up my mind I'm going after God, I told my old friends God dealing with me and I'm gone let him have his way in my life God took the smoke out my mouth, I found myself one-day that I didn't say a curse word all that day, I stop Fornicating I was taught coming in The harvest you can't have sex and say you saved, I told my job take me off the schedule for Sundays, I told my manger I go to Church, I had learned that Sabbath is supposed to be the Lord day, we supposed to do dedicate the Sabbath day to do the Lord. I wanted to do right by God and change, Because I knew that the Lord was with my Leaders and they was speaking Truth.

One Word That Arch Bishop James Rice spoke before that stuck with me and I hold it to my heart I want let it go, He said (WHY GO BACK TO WHAT YOU ALREADY TRIED) That stuck with me, I know that the things I tried and been threw wasn't working for me I knew what it caused me, I realized that when he said that, this is my opportunity to get it right and don't go back to (WHAT I ALREADY TRIED)

Greater Harvest has been A blessing in my life, A leader who got saved at 20years old Just like me to have Leaders that has walk this walk with GOD for 30+Years Living Holy, Love there Sheep,

Teaching Sound Doctrine, Walk in the Apostolic, The 5fold Ministry, Has Compassion, Are Educated, Leadership Builders, Christian Counselors, And They Are Blessed Ambassadors. What God has gave me is his Greatest Gift, A Spiritual Father Bishop James Rice, He has been a Father to me that I hope for has counsel me, taught me about the difference between King And Street Boy, My Bishop is Man Of God Full Of Wisdom, Ideas, And Dreams, Who Love God, His Wife, And His Church

Watching Bishop I seen what's a real Father, He also pour a lot in my husband Michael Thompson he is a Role Model in my Husband Life Who My Husband Look up to. I thank my Spiritual Father for being a Father to me And teaching me How to Love God, Love Myself, And Forgive people Daily And Like We Say In The Harvest We LOVE OUR BISHOP OH YES WE DO!! Being a part of Greater Harvest Was What I Need! I Learn so much as my Leaders has taught us is when we get a word we have to that word in apply it to our life When I begin To apply the word to my life and walk in it God begin to un-blind my eyes I started to see different, I taught to follow, swallow, and obey When you follow the order of the and Obey the Prophet, God want let you down, God has help me got threw when I didn't understand as I was Being taught.

My Spiritual Mother Chief-Apostle Dr. J G Rice has taught me how to dress in the house God, when I was lazy didn't want to fix my hair coming in the church with my hair any kind of way Apostle was the only person who cared how I look, How keep my kids nice, She took the time out to teach me how to become a Woman, A Mother I thought what I was doing was okay, when I was walking in the same old me like I was Nobody, Was dressing like I was in the streets, She seen something in me that I couldn't see.

I finally got a Mother, A Leader, A Mentor Somebody that care about want to sec me go some-where the things she have done for she really didn't have to do. When took the time out to Mentor me teach I seen things Different she open my eyes to so much, How to be real and don't be moved by people, And to do God's

Work I can't Reject it I watch her do Kingdom Work, Take Care Husband, Take care of her Home, Take care of her Sheep, Take time to Mentor her sheep, Praise God Daily And Don't Complain Nor make Excuses. She lets Me Know That All Things Are Possible Threw Christ Jesus Who Strengthen You!! By Summiting Myself and follow the order of the house, I have seen Miracles in my life And having the Favor Of God on My life

At 7 months being in Ministry I preach My first service, I am being train in Leadership, God has bless me with a 2 bed-room 2 bath Apartment , A car, God has Bless me with a Husband After His Heart, And Who Love His Leaders, His Wife, And Kids I am being equip to do Kingdom Work and Working On My Salvation God has bless me up under the Leaders Of Chief-Apostle Dr. J G Rice And Arch Bishop James Rice And The 2nd Degree Felony That I Caught In Went To Jail For God Has Saved Me from 15 years Of prison And I Am Not Convicted When nobody wouldn't come to court My Spiritual Mother And Father was right by side And That's Why I WANT GO BACK CAN'T GO BACK TO THE WAY I USE TO BE!!

For Every-One Who Is Reading My Story-My Testimony Of What God Has Brought Me Out Of
I was born with a spot on my brain that was cancer. Yes, I Was molested many times, I was Raped, I was Abused, I was Lied-On, Felt Abandoned, I was By-Sexual, I was A smoker, I Held A Secret Of My Uncle C until I was 20 years old Had a Mother On Drugs, My Dad Was In Out My Life, I Sold Drugs, I Was A Fighter I Been Arrested 3 times, I Clubbed, I Drank, And Stayed And Other People Problems.

Through all of that God kept me, When they said I was Nobody God said I was Somebody. I used to say "You Can't Tell Me Nothing I'm Grown." Now I say "You Can't Tell Me Who I Am, I Know Where I'm Growing In Christ Jesus."Old things has pass away, And I am a New Creature In Christ Jesus. I Encourage You To LET GO AND LET GOD COME IN YOUR HEART. Now That Jesus Has Chosen Me I'm Looking At My Future And Its Looking Mighty Good.

UPDATE...

"To all those reading at the time of the printing of this testimonial, my story continues. To no fault of my leaders, that encouraged myself and my husband to wait we decided to marry anyway. We both had a lot of "RATISM" to overcome. This led to separations and finally a divorce, also against the advice of our leaders. I soon learned that failed instruction leads to destruction, as our Archbishop James Rice teaches. While overlooking I noticed I was hot headed and so was my former spouse. Longer I thought the longer my list showed my failures which I have repented, have been forgiven of, and restored to my happy place with God. However my story goes on and I am still saved, praising God, and serving my church faithfully. To God be the Glory, great things he STILL continues to do in my life.

Thanks for sharing my journey with me. I love and respect my leaders more for their unbiased support, truth, and spiritual, spirit filled counseling. What did I learn? Chief Apostle Dr J G RICE and Archbishop James Rice of Greater Harvest Christian Center Churches Worldwide- IGACCW always asks us this. I have learned we have leadership in our lives for a reason, as well as if we are going to take the time to be mentored that we are to use, and apply the advice provided to you. " LET WISDOM HAVE ITS PERFECT WORK IN YOUR LIFE" is a constant word I stand on. I purpose to apply my leaders wisdom now, for out of them flow the rivers of life, experiences, and truth!"

LOVE EVANGELIST MARIAH MASON

CHAPTER 7

58 FACTORS TO SUCCESS AND TRANSFORMATION

FACTORS
1 THROUGH 23

SKILLS
Factors 1-9

Skills are defined as proficiencies in an art or craft. Being that this is the basic definition for skill, we must acknowledge the point of first becoming proficient. Then developing this proficiency in an art or craft. You just don't "fall" into being skillful. You must work passionately in a defined area or areas, until your become good in it.

This factor of "Good" should then be made "Great" and then "Excellent." Make up your mind to develop at least one new skill per month.

What skills are willing to start developing this month?

I will develop this skill this month:

_____

I will develop this skill next month :

_____

Factor 1: Access the Hidden

You have "Hidden and Open" skills. Skills you have not yet forced yourself to tap into. Acknowledging this is the start to a new mindset.

To change or challenge your old mindset, you must tap into your higher skill levels. Don't be a pansy, do something new.

Challenge yourself to learn and do something new this week. To access your "Hidden and Open" skills.

You will impress yourself with your new ability! If you are afraid to try new things alone, enlist a partner to roll with you on this journey, and both of you will grow to newer heights and fulfill many of your dreams.

Factor 2: Motivate Yourself

Motivation of one's self is the greatest tool to finding out your new skills. Talk about yourself positively! You are not a failure!

There is something you do great, so talk about it and purpose to add it to the list of these great things.... everyday.... every year. Soon there will be a lot of things you enjoy, are passionate about, and are skillful in.

This will change your inner worth and job/society worth, guaranteeing you a greater paycheck and an overall well feeling about yourself.

Factor 3: Bargains in life - vs - Cheap life

Learn to seek out great bargains, versus being cheap. A skillful shopper/ investor is a gainful person. Cheap is a loud way of saying I have no Shopping Skills. Versus Bargain saying I have the ability to select great products at a minimum price.

Factor 4: Try to do it yourself FIRST

Instead of paying someone for minor jobs, try to do it yourself first. This will greatly increase your skill levels. Take a "How To" class if you need to. There are many classes available that will save you thousands of dollars. How to paint a room. How to change a door knob. How to plant a garden.

You can greatly be rewarded by doing small projects yourself. And your confidence level will never be the same as you review your great work, and others admire your skills.

Factor 5: Operate in new things

What are 3 things you do well?

1._____
2._____
3._____

What are 3 things you would like to do well?

1._____
2._____
3._____

Can you learn how to do these things NOW? ___ Yes ___No

Where? _____

How? _____

Cost? _____

Time? _____

Well then, let's get started. We all can learn to operate in new things. This is called additional skill development. Every year you should have 2 new skills that you have developed to continue to allow your mind to grow and enrich your overall wellbeing.

What is your new skill going to be this month?

_____

Factor 6: Dare to go where you have not been before!

This mentality is the greatest of all mental skills. Having a "No Fear" mentality to try new things and develop new skills. You are never too old, too young, too short or too tall.

Disabilities should not stop you either. Look at every person whom could use every excuse that you have used, yet they developed new skills and conquered every fear. And the end result...Victory! Don't let your lack cause you to slack. God has empowered you to succeed. Now go for it!

Factor 7: Be Teachable

Over the years I have encountered several persons who said they wanted to learn something but were very un-teachable. Or who lacked the ability to be taught.

When you lose the ability to be taught, you lose the ability to learn new skills. You must have an "Open Mind" to learn new skills. I knew a person who had been in the nursing field for over 35 years and retired for more than 25 years. We were talking about a new medical practice, but this nurse was un-teachable, saying she knew more about medicine that we did.

She was right, but we knew more about this procedure than she did. You see, this procedure has only been around for 7 years, and she has long since retired. Failing to go back to school and enhance her skill level had made her past levels of experience null and void.

You must remain teachable. Every day something new is being revealed to us that seek to know new things. Yesterday's knowledge is sometimes void. Becoming teachable will keep your skills sharp and your mindset open for higher gains.

Factor 8: Trigger a New Mindset

Triggering a new mindset means to make your mind do something that it has never thought of, or done before. A trigger is something that makes your light bulb come on, like this book. Thinking on a "new meal" to eat, going to a "new place" to see, or experiencing a new adventure. All this and more can trigger a new mindset.

A mindset is what you have set your mind to do. Sometimes this is very limited. Limited to what you can see, hear, feel, taste, and your personal experiences. When you challenge your personal senses to experience new things, your mindset shifts and elevates and expands, if you will.

Prepare to trigger a new mindset for yourself. Read a new magazine and try to embrace a new thought that will also trigger a new mindset for you. These new mindsets will challenge you to greater skill levels.

Factor 9: Get a Bigger Ruler

You cannot measure yourself by yourself. This practice of judging oneself by oneself can only bring a reading that is untrue and unmerited. If you are to access your skill level, you must find at least 22 other persons in which you can be measured by. This will give you a fair starting point at which to access yourself. Always remember, you could be the fastest runner in your town, but your town only has 10 people. This will not make you the fastest runner in the world.

When measuring your skill level be fair to yourself and others. Find out who and what is out there, and measure by a bigger ruler. Then you can truly rank your skills fairly.

Summary

- ❖ Embrace every new possibility with passion, grace, and enthusiasm. Do not put yourself in a box.

- ❖ You can increase your skill level daily, weekly, monthly, and yearly.

- ❖ Your mindset must be changed to from closed to " Open" in order to continue to grow and embrace new things, ideals, and skills.

- ❖ You have "Hidden and Open skills," tap into them!

- ❖ Creating new skills will increase your life, health, mental views and family stability.

- ❖ Be teachable and be determined to experience life learning new skills and doing new things.

- ❖ You have great skills. Re-sharpen when necessary to stay on the cutting edge. **A dull knife is no good.**

- ❖ You are created by the most skillful God, and great skills are in you… Do not fear…develop your skills.

UNDERSTANDING
Factors 10-13

"Above ALL your getting, get an understanding." This famous quote of proverbs is most said and seldom understood. The word "understanding" being two joined words with different meanings forms to make a powerful statement.

Under = beneath, covered by, the subject of
Standing = to maintain an upright position and or attitude, a designated position.

Combined meaning: to "stand under." This makes us search ourselves as to what we are really standing under or submitting to in our beliefs and directions in life. So above all, (rephrased) "Make sure to agree with and can support what you are standing under."

Understanding = "To comprehend, to believe to be the case, to support, to know the nature and character of"

Having said this, Understanding should be the essence in which our lives can be developed and groomed.

Factor 10: Get to know yourself

Yes, get to know and understand yourself (better). Do you really know you?

List 3 things you really know about yourself?

1._____
2._____
3. _____

How do these things make you feel about yourself?

_____

_____

_____

_____

Do you understand your ways? _____ *Yes* _____ *No*

Who in your family do you act like?

_____

Who do people attribute your character to?

_____

What are your greatest
*fears?*_____

_____

_____

When you understand you, you can help others understand you better. Then you can create a "Happy" atmosphere for yourself and others to enjoy, as they to enjoy you.

Factor 11: It's A New Day

Understand that every day is a new day. A fresh start. Hope is new today. Dreams and goals are new today. The breath of life is new today. You must embrace the newness of the day to receive the best of the day.

Learn from the mistakes of yesterday and move on. Only embrace the positive, blow out the negative, and **BREATH AGAIN**. "This to will pass." You will do better tomorrow than you did today!

Factor 12: Get the Answer

Learn the Solution, not the Problem. The Answer is not in the problem. Everyone can talk about the problem, but who can solve the problem. Problem solvers are few and far. **If you can get an Understanding that you are here on earth to solve the problems, not be a problem, than you will have great success.**

Everyone will not like you as a problem solver, but you will sleep great at night. You will also get rid of lots of negative people who only want to talk about the problems of life. "WOE IS ME" people will soon fade out of your life and you will understand that the greatest good is to speak the solutions and not problems.

Factor 13: Understand the real meaning of work

You must understand that the real meaning to work is the ability to learn **New** and be **Promoted** in things. You must work to learn, not work for money. The more you learn the more you will understand. The more you understand, the more your increase will be.

Your purpose for going to work is to learn. You must pick up additional understanding and skills to be successful in life. Understand that life presents opportunities every day to give you a better life and added fulfillment.

Summary

❖ When you set yourself up for greatness, You must add understanding to your arsenal of learning.

❖ You must know yourself… better than anything, and anybody… You must be honest with yourself and your vision.

❖ Understanding that you are sent as a solution to the problem. You are an answer to the situation… See yourself as an answer.

❖ You are called to cultivate your spiritual reserves, and tap into your potential to understand and to be understood.

❖ The greatest gift is the gift of understanding. Love it and embrace it… and you will have success.

CREATIVITY
Factors 14-18

See these wonderful flowers behind this picture? Guess what, I made them! And they are proudly a part of our sanctuary. Someone quoted me a price of $300.00 for this type of flower arrangement, plus the cost of the container. Well I made this arrangement for $37.00 total, including the cost of the container. Am I a flower designer? No. But I do have creativity, and so do you.

Creativity flows through our veins. Just trust yourself to begin your journey of creativity and see the dynamic results. You will impress yourself. I did!

Factor 14: A clear vision brings Creativity

To be creative you must have a clear vision and a direct flow to see yourself in the blossom of life. To have a "Clear Vision" you must be a seer. Vision is the ability to SEE clearly and directly, and to be able to communicate your vision well.

This takes planning and development of your written skills and your verbal ability. Work on this and your vision will be expressed as you desire.

Factor 15: Commit to Excellence

To be creative you must decide that " just enough" is not good enough. You must commit to be excellent and to do the " BEST" you possibly can. Creativity flows when things are done right. **You cannot side-step excellence and expect to be creative.** You must decide that your product is the best and that you continue to want to be the BEST.

Factor 16: Maximize Time

Don't be a time waster. Use your time wisely and efficiently. Get a day planner or a sheet of paper and see where the time in your day is really going. You would be surprised at the areas where you can pick up valuable minutes, which turns into hours, weeks, months, and years.

Time cannot ever be regained, but it can be retrained. Start today by being fair to yourself and learn to say **NO** to invaluable time wasters.

Factor 17: Remember to DREAM BIG!

Dream Big! The sky is truly the limit. If you can see it, You CAN achieve it. There is not a lot to it. Seeing " It" allows creativity to begin and to grow!

Meditate on the " Project," Goal," and "Dream" you want to accomplish and do it from start to completion. There is nothing wrong with dreaming. Without a dream you will die. Focus on your end result until it becomes a reality.

List five things you use to do that were creative and enjoyable, and you've stopped doing them and why.

1. I use to:

_____

I stopped because

_____

2. I use to:

_____

I stopped because

_____

3. I use to:

_____

I stopped because

_____

4. I use to:

_____

I stopped
*because*_____

5. I use to:

_____

I stopped
*because*_____

Factor 18: Creativity is a FLOW!

Think of being as creative as a " River." It is a flow and must have a constant flowing to continue to be active an effective. Get rid of "River Stoppers." Beavers who hinder your creative process, and unwanted elements that might deter your " River Flow."

Who/ What can you eliminate first ?

_____

Summary

❖ Learn as much as you can about your dream.

❖ Ask questions, join associations, improve your learning and knowledge about the area you want to be creative in.

❖ Dream again and dream big! Don't allow anyone to stop your flow of creativity. God has given you a dream and no one has the right to change, deter, or stop it.

❖ **You have the right to get rid of all dream killer and vision stealers!**

❖ Take time to **Meditate** and settle your mind to focus on GOOD things. This will help you define and develop your creativity and skills.

<u>CHOICES</u>
FACTORS 19-23

Life provides us with a multitude of choices that can be made. Having negative things in our lives have created a recycling of wrong choices. You must put yourself on a schedule to change your focus and choices. This is a practical plan that if followed, will bring you to a point of positive choices.

It is your choice to get Better, to do Better, to be Stronger, and to live Longer. You can change everything, by starting today.

You and God are the only two entities with the ability and power to change your situation. The choice you make today will determine your tomorrow. What is your choice? Change or Not?

List one item you will change TODAY :

_____

How will you change this item?
I plan to

_____

<u>Factor 19: Learn to forget the Old</u>

Learn to forget the old. All the negative situations and events, and **Embrace the New**. All positive situations and events that make you smile and grow. Tell yourself every day that you are made in the image of Excellence, and that NOTHING will effect or influence that image.

You must release all bad thoughts. This can be done by

thinking on new bright things. For 5 minutes per day just close your eyes and focus on the color yellow, or whatever your favorite color is. And say 5 positive things about the choices you made that day.

The Good CHOICES I made today were…

1.

2.

3.

4.

5.

Factor 20: Retrain your Mouth

Retrain your vocabulary. Constantly get rid of negative(s)

1) People
2) Things
3) Ideals

Reevaluate often, and don't be afraid to toss out the negative. It is important to your choices to learn what is good and what is bad for you. Only you can really make this powerful decision. When you know it's bad, get rid of it. If someone or something causes you to not have control of your vocabulary, they are probably negative in other areas and need to be "trained" or "tossed out."

Put three Good things in your vocabulary daily that you will say about yourself.

I am _____

I am _____

I am _____

Factor 21: Talk About YOU!

You must make the choice to talk about yourself and say good things about yourself and to yourself. Also make the choice to stop others from saying negative things about you to you.

You do not have to entertain people how are verbally abusive and negative to you, neither should you buy into their negative comments about you. Talk about your goals and dreams. Tell your audience that you are great and there are good things about you. To do this you must believe this about yourself.

List three good things about yourself, so that you can share them with others .

_____

_____

Factor 22: Get a "TEAM"

Get people to be on your personal team. Meet with them monthly, and talk positively about the New You. Where you are going and your new goals and personal improvements to motivate yourself. Find 4 people and share your dreams with them.

T= Talker
E=Educator
A= Active Supporter
M= Mentor

Factor 23: Life is like a Refrigerator

Clean your "Life Refrigerator" often. Make a choice to get rid of "old, dead, spoiled, depleted, contaminated, rotten , freezer burned" areas in your life. This will make room for the "new, fresh, enriched, healthy, nutritious and beneficial" areas that will be added unto you as you continue on your journey towards TRANSFORMATION.

SUMMARY

❖ Life is full of choices, Good and Bad… WE must reprogram our thoughts to secure good choices in our life.

❖ Retrain your mouth to speak positives about yourself. Remove all negative thoughts, people and things from around you.

❖ Say good things about yourself. Believe in yourself.

❖ We must get a personal team that we can share our dreams with and that will motivate us forward.

❖ When cleaning your life refrigerator, use good cleaning products that disinfect and kill contaminations.

Good Disinfectants

Pine-sol = Praise and Worship. Find a good joyous song to sing and sing it. It will brighten your day.

Bleach = The word of God. Find a good positive scripture to enrich and brighten your choices. You will feel so much better about the choices your make when you know it is the will of God.

Air Freshener (s) = Other good and positive books that help you to make good solid choices.

CHAPTER
8

LETTING
GO

MY NAME IS KENDRA BAILEY. I WAS
MENTALLY, EMOTINALLY AND SEXUALLY
ABUSED I USED THE "58 FACTORS TO SUCCESS
AND TRANSFORMATION" TO CHANGE MY LIFE.
HERE IS MY STORY...

KENDRA BAILEY

Before I was introduced to the ministry my life was an emotional roller coaster. I would be up, down, whirlwind around, tossed to and fro. It started when I was about four years old when my step father died. I could remember little clips of him but not enough to understand why he was gone. After he died my mother who was taking care of my great aunt's daughter, my sister, and I would soon split us apart. My cousin, who I though was my sister then and I was sent off to live with our aunt while our youngest sister stayed with her. My aunt was already raising her sister's children because she had died when her children were very small. She also had four children of her own; so in total there were nine of us in a three bedroom duplex. My aunt was very strict and mean at times. See I was spoiled rotten by my mom and step father so when I moved with my aunt everything was different. We all attended the same elementary school about a block away, so we all would leave the house and come back at the same time. We had to do our homework, clean, eat dinner, and go to bed; in that order. On the weekends, sometimes my mom would come and see my sister and I; we still didn't know we were cousins. I don't remember spending much time with my mother, I just would cry and beg her not to leave me because I didn't want to stay with my aunt. There were things going on that she had no idea about. When I was five years old one of my older girl cousins would wake me up in the middle of the night because she liked to touch me in the bathtub. I already knew about breast and vagina because I would see it all the time. One particular night my aunt caught her, and told me to get to bed; she never touched me again after that.

Eventually, my mother came to get me, by this time I was in the first grade. I attended elementary school and breezed through with amazing teachers and friends to help me along the way. We lived with my grandmother, along with my uncle and step grandfather. There are actually more happier memories than sad ones. After my sister and I would leave school, we would attend after school care at Bass Park Recreation Center. We were involved in cheerleading, ballet dance, soccer, soft ball, tennis, girls scouts; and any other extracurricular activity that was available there. We didn't have much, but we wed happy the most when we stayed busy. This was our home away from home, even though it was right up the block from my grandmother's house. During these years, our family was full of unity. So when we weren't at the camp, we took family trips, there were big parties: birthdays, holidays, etc. However, it would always be arguing and fighting along with drugs and alcohol; which was the norm for us. When I experienced the first family fight, it was sad, I didn't want my family to fight we would cry because it wasn't right. But after a while I got used to it, and started helping. I could remember a rampage of people walking around the corner when we were having a family get together at my grandmother's house. I really don't know how it started but my family finished the altercation. People were jumping on cars, and braking windows; people were screaming, cursing, bleeding and carrying on. So I grew up on the basis of drugs, alcohol, fighting, cursing; all at a young age. Nothing was off limits, we had access to everything. The adults were present but they weren't watchful, they had their party and we had ours; anything goes. We would sneak beer and cigarettes, porn tapes; whatever we got our hands on that we knew children were not supposed to have. We lived with my grandmother up until I was in the fifth grade, after my mom got married to my stepfather.

So these attractions for me carried on to middle school but they got worse. I kept good grades in school but I acted out when I was home because I was able to get away with more of what I wanted to do. Mostly I wanted to be home where the boys were because they gave me attention. I loved the attention and liked to have sex by any means necessary. My first time was with a guy that I barely knew. He was supposed to be the cool guy in the neighborhood. I thought he liked me, I was twelve and he was sixteen, all my cousins were pushing me to go out with him because he was so cute. In the meantime there was this guy that I was dating who never kissed me unless I asked him to, he barely touched me. I took advantage of that and let this guy take the only precious think I had at the time but I was trying to be cool. He walked me around the corner from my aunt's house I thought we were just going to the store but when we walked to the back of the store, he asked me to lay down on the ground and asked me if I loved him. He said that he loved me and we were going to have sex right behind the convenient store; so we did and it was very painful. It took about five minutes at the most because I told him to stop, he did and he walked me back to my aunt's house; I never saw him again! After spilling the news to my cousins they all laughed at me and eventually my mother found out. She didn't beat me, she just cried and that was the year when she didn't buy me anything for my birthday. She told me since I was grown, she wasn't going to buy me anything. Everyone knew what had happened, but my aunt who I lived with years before was there to tell me everyone gets into trouble so move along and don't feel sorry for myself. I was so mad at my cousin because she promised not to tell on me; we didn't speak for weeks.

After this incident blew over, I actually had gotten worse. My grades stayed the same but my attitude was horrible. I started talking sassy to my mother and fighting with my sisters and little brother. At the age of thirteen I met a guy who lived next door to us he was seventeen at the time we started dating. My mom didn't agree with it in the beginning but eventually she came around. We stayed together for as long as three years while I was involved with the guy around the corner, a guy at school, and around where my aunt stayed. I had to have variety; I was never happy with one person. I had men in my life as father figures, but the only father I thought I knew was dead, and my biological father was in prison half my life. I don't ever remember spending time with my real dad, and I grew to not care so much about his existence. As I grew up a little more, school got a lot less interesting and boys became my focal point. Hundreds of them were in and out my bedroom, it's like I was a sex magnet. Over time I didn't care if they had girlfriends or not I just needed a quick fix. I played many games with these boys, because no one took me serious. It's like when I wanted to be seriously in a relationship with a guy he was either too slow for me or took full advantage. I had sex in cars, at the beach, on the playground, in the hospital; wherever I didn't care about myself but I didn't realize it.

There were also internal damages for my performance. My cousins were supposed to be there to protect me from boys that wanted to have sex with me. But how could they do this when they wanted to have sex with me themselves. The boys would come and stay the night at my Mom's house and when we went to sleep at night, there was definitely some touching and rubbing going on. In the day time my older cousin was supposed to watch us but we were playing house. I can remember him putting his fingers in me; he asked and I said yes. It was hurting really bad, and it burned. Another one would try and pull my clothes down when we stayed over to my aunt's house, but he was never successful with raping me because we were always in the house with lots of people. I told him if he'd try to rape me that I was scream and let the adults know what was going on. He laughed at me and let me go. He would go on to have sex forcefully with most of the young girls in my family, taking some of their virginity. The girls had sex with each other as well.

Everything stopped internally after my family members started dying. My aunt dies leaving her and her sisters children; which she kept the family together. So when she passed away everyone either moved away or stopped talking. Her brother died shortly after she did, and her daughter dies five years later. There were no more family parties, each time our family reunion came around, no one would attend; there was so much division. In high school I leaned to my friends for comfort because they were positive people in my life at the time. My promiscuous days were over because it had gotten old I was wore out. But I had developed serious trust issues over time. I met my husband in the eleventh grade and from the first time we met he was a sweet heart. He never took advantage of me, he told me I was pretty, he was very respectful to my mom and the rest of my family. I could be myself with him. I also still had the " I don't care mentality", so I cheated on him. I stringed him along with all the games and guys that I was involved with. We broke up and didn't get together until after I left college. But before I went off to college I had a son at the age of seventeen, I didn't have to take care of him because my mom did. I started drinking and smoking, going out to the clubs and staying overnight with guys. I was a terrible mother. So before I got worse, my mother sent me off to college.

During college, I was alone and bored in the beginning because I never stayed on campus. My mom did whatever she had to do in order for me to make it there. It didn't last because I eventually hooked up with a local guy where I attended college and was hooked back to drugs and the club. After calling my mom when he choked me out and I had lost my apartment, she sent money to me so that I can come back home. Soon I saw an old friend on Facebook who was a member of this church. Now this was surprising because I knew who he was when we attended the same middle school. While I was in college I tried a church and was involved in different ministries: culinary, music, children's church, and youth night; but I wasn't dedicated so I ran. This led to me dropping out of college and getting a part time job back at home. I was now a full-time mom; which me and my son really didn't have a close bond because I didn't take care of him and I left to attend college. I was working minimum wage, and helping my mother with needs around the house.

After finally giving the fast life up, I became a member of Greater Harvest Christian Center. Today I have been a member for about two years and striving for better. I have learned to pardon those that have done me wrong by forgiving them. I never thought that I would be married and working full time making more money than I have ever made in my life. I am learning how to be trustworthy and faithful in the ministry with the teaching and counseling that I am receiving from the Chief Apostle and Arch Bishop Rice. They are showing me true love and discipline; the two most valuable things that I have been lacking my entire life. I had to make tough decisions like leaving my family behind and saying no when they want things or ask me to do things that I shouldn't do. I am learning how to use my mind instead of my body; I'm learning to love myself again. Through fellowship and worship, fasting and praying; God is bringing me back to where I belong. I thank God for giving me another chance to get my mind right! I appreciate the man and woman of God, the Angels that God has placed in my life to watch over my soul, will, and emotions. I can't make it on my own, and I need someone to guide me in the righteous direction for the rest of my life. I know eventually I will have to be like the baby eagle and get kicked out of the nest to fly on my own, but I want to not only receive but catch as much wisdom knowledge and understanding as I can. If you haven't gotten anything from my story, know that I am still fighting this fight, and I didn't give up. I encourage young woman to be the best you, you can be; not what somebody wants you to be. Get into a ministry where you know the un-compromised Word of God is being taught and stick through it; "only what you do for God will last" is what I'm being taught at the Harvest.

CHAPTER 9

58 POINTS TO SUCCESS AND TRANSFORMATION

FACTORS
24 THROUGH 40

EDUCATIONAL ENRICHMENT
Factors 24-30

"Education is about control, and control is about education." Education allows you to make better choices and decisions.

Take 71 Days to change your life!

This plan for "Learning to make the best Choices" should be done in 1 week intervals to re-develop the way you chose and make choices, about learning, growing, gleaming and setting smarter. It will enrich your life. Do each point for one week, saturating yourself in the principles that will make yourself successful.

7 weeks to educational enrichment!

Factor 24: Plan to Educate Yourself

Educate yourself to where you want to go! Take one week to enhance yourself with new educational goals. Plan to take a short course or a semester to enhance your knowledge in one area.

When do you start…

Factor 25: Educate your family

Tell them your plans, goals, and directions. Tell them your dreams and how they can help. Tell them your expectations. Tell your family how they fit into your educational concepts. Give your children/ spouse/ family a part in your dream and goals (if you can). Or give them additional responsibility to help (household chores) so you can gain your new educational goals.

Factor 26: Educate your Inner Circle/Friends/ Social

Train your friends. Tell them your goals and see whose willing to help your SUCCEED.

Factor 27: Educate your Target Market

Educate yourself to your target Market. Learn whose out there, who do what you want to do, and who you can partner with. If you're planning to start a new business then, plan to start a new business. What do you want to do? When do your start?

Factor 28: Educate the World

Find out how to send yourself to the World. Develop yourself as a business person. Get some type of business started. Develop business Cards, web sites, and invest in "Personal Development" classes. **The world is ready to hear about you**. But if you cannot go to the world at least go to your family, friends and social friends and introduce your business.

Factor 29: Invest in Continued Personal Enrichment

I cannot stress this enough. Take one week to personally enrich yourself. Your clothing, hair, and style should reflect your upcoming business. Getting better personally will enrich your life. **Spend money on educating yourself**. This must be added to your budget and not seen as a maybe or possibility, but as a mandate to your future growth.

Factor 30: Get Legal

Take 10 days to learn the practical business applications that may apply to your particular business. Educate yourself to what you need to be legally licensed, State and Federal regulations, and if necessary, all City Licenses. Take a Business Start Up Class. Find one, and if you are serious about changing your future, take it. No Excuses! **TAKE IT!**

SUMMARY

- ❖ Education is the force that will enrich your life … your happiness… your dreams… and your goals.

- ❖ You must love Education and Education will Love you.

- ❖ Embrace Change and strive to learn something NEW EVERYDAY!

- ❖ Educate your family (immediate and distant) as you educate yourself.

- ❖ Plan to know more next month than you knew this month.

- ❖ Invest in continued personal enrichment courses and classes.
- ❖ Attend seminars, workshops and school to enrich yourself and challenge your mental mindset.

- ❖ Use your new education to Start a Business. Plan it, believe it, and achieve it. A new you starts with an educated and expanded mind. Plan to stretch your mind today!

SUPERNATURAL ENERGY AND HEALTH FACTORS 31-34

"You cannot be the Best if your health is not the best."

For years I went my merry way constipated and loving it. Yes, I said it, CONSTIPATED! My colon was a mess, therefore my body was a mess. My mind and energy, yes you guessed it, was a mess too.
You see if your colon is not working properly, than you are at risk for low energy, low focus, low everything. And eventually everything else goes bad.

Next to our skin, the intestines are the next largest organ in the body. And when it does not function property you gain other problems. Some people are on medicine and they really only need a good cleaning out. Go see a "colon specialist" (I prefer a Natural Health Specialist) and find out what you are really full of.

Factor 31: Feelings do matter

When you feel good, you do good. No matter how you try to trick others , only you know if you really feel good. Some of us have settled for poor health so long that we really do not know when we feel good.

Take me for example me, (I rarely talk about me), I felt bad for so long that I did not know that felt bad until I felt better. I started with 3 Colonics, and then I realized that I felt bad before I had them. Afterwards, I felt light, energetic, and ready to go. Then I began an intestinal health revitalization program for myself. After 6 months my waistline dropped 3 sizes, My breath was "Sweet," my eyes were better, my joints hurt less, I got out of bed quicker, and I was a much happier person.

I firmly believe I helped the Lord add 15 years to my life. I never knew I was supposed to go to the bathroom so much. I encourage everyone to check on their colon health, and add years to their lives and happiness to their family.

Factor 32: Skip one meal a week

Going back to Eden for your food diet will not hurt you at all. Try to eliminate one meal from your regular diet a week. Giving your intestines a break, to catch up and digest other foods. Add vegetables, fruits, nuts, grains, and whole wheat to your diet. This will increase your health and your life.

One hand full of nuts a week will help your digestion and health. Also, consult the Bible. Deuteronomy Chapter 14 and Leviticus Chapter 11 may add to your healthy eating plan.

Factor 33: Add salt to your Ministry, not to your life!

Try to use a whole lot less salt. Salt is the one thing used for preservatives, and it allows excessive fluid to build up in your body and inhibits your ability to release toxins as you should. Extra salt affects blood sugar, blood pressure, and many other physical elements.
Why is it so hard to lose the extra Salt? We don't believe salt is killing the human body. But it is.

When I was recovering from surgery and finally started eating, I could taste the natural salt in everything, even eggs. I would say to my beloved Husband, "don't put so much salt in the food," and to my dismay he hadn't added any. I learned recently the amount of salt in a packet of ketchup and other condiments. I suggest to you to get the flyers from restaurants about their individual food preparations and learn the salt percentage. This will be your beginning to a healthier life.

Factor 34: Water is Life and Exercise is POWER!

Drinking water is the beginning of great health. After all, your body is mostly made of water. When you are dehydrated you are not giving your body the needed water to survive on. This does not mean soda, energy drinks, or other liquid additives. Your body needs water and exercise.

Exercise will strengthen your muscles, your mind, and give you supernatural energy. My God Mother (MTR) is 76 and an avid exerciser and in great health and shape, really great shape. She attributes this to water and exercise. I believe her and strive to reach her exercise routine.

SUMMARY

❖ We all want to live longer, so we must do something to create healthy habits, these habits include Water and Exercise.

❖ Water is the <u>Spring of Life</u>, and Exercise will strength your body to
❖ get you to the water you need.

❖ You must eat better. Healthy eating is a key to supernatural health. Skip one meal per week and give your body a chance to catch up. It will increase your life by 10 years.

❖ Make sure you pay close attention to your intestinal health. Keep your colon clean and fresh to help process food, give you energy, and brighten your day.

❖ Get outdoors. Do something outdoors at least once every 9 days, once a week is better. Rake the yard, plant a garden, sit on the steps and read a book.

❖ Doing something outside will increase your oxygen and improve your lungs. Go to the park, take a nature trail walk, just get outdoors.

SPIRITUAL IDENTITY
Factors 35-40

"When you know the CREATOR you can understand the CREATION better . The CREATOR is God and the CREATION is you."

It's plain and simple, we did not create ourselves or come from a big bang theory. We were not an accident. We were created by a loving Creator who did not make a mistake or error. It is wonderful and great to know that God so loved us that He breathed his very breath in us and gave us life.

Therefore knowing this gives us the power to succeed, and become a SUCCESS. Therefore as we get to understand and receive our creator, we understand and receive ourselves.

God is great…	And so are WE
God is Love….	And so are WE
God is powerful…	And so are WE
God is abundant…	And so are WE

Do you get the picture…?

Factor 35: "One Creator" makes us all valuable

I believe in MY worth and the value of others. Therefore I respect all life and every person and creation of the Creator God. This respect will lead me to knowing other persons better and realizing that they have value a well. It will lead me to conversations that will allow me to see the goodness in others. I will constantly try to find something good in others, as I show them the good that is in me. Therefore showing the value of God the creator, in me his creation.

I am Like the Creator in the 5 following Ways:

1._____

2._____

3._____

4._____

5._____

Factor 36: God Cares For me

God is on my side. He loves me and cares for me. Yes, I have the embracing care of God. He cares for me, my wellbeing, my thoughts, and the direction my life goes.

It does not always make sense to me that everything does not work as I think or plan. But be certain that God loves you and cares for you. Be patient with the plans you have and meditate on good thoughts. And you will begin to see the creators plan for you.

Factor 37: It's in what you say

Confess positive scriptures about your health, wellbeing, finances, mindset, and spiritual growth. You say it, you will do it. You do it, you will become it. You WILL achieve it.

Factor 38: Get on a Journey to go somewhere

Go from " I can't" to "I can." It's a beautiful journey that will take you to your point of excellence.

You might be able to do a lot of things, but when you realize that the statement " I can do something" is an inactive statement of purpose. But " I am doing something" is an active statement.

Make up in your mind to change this statement at least 2 times per month

I Am now doing _____

I Am now doing _____

Factor 39: I Love to Serve Others

When I learned that the best gift is giving I gave more, and therefore received the best gift of all. Serving others has led me to be blessed myself. The greatest joy is the joy of helping someone else reach their destiny and their dreams. Giving them what I have already learned enhances me with God and mankind.

Factor 40: I Love LIFE

I am grateful to my creator for my life and will not waste it for any reason. My life is valuable and is set for purpose. If I do not know my purpose I will seek a counselor of God, a Life Coach or a Personal Advisor to help me find my purpose.

I purpose to live my life happy and with the joy of the Creator who I embrace with gratitude for this. My good life!

SUMMARY

❖ You are the best "YOU" the creator has ever made. He molded you for SUCCESS and divine development. As you become one with the Creator you will become one with yourself.

❖ You have everything it takes to make it work. Meditate on the good points in your life and refresh yourself daily with the good thoughts that the Creator God has for you. As these thoughts become a pattern in your life you will see them materialize and allow you to become a great You inside of YOU.

❖ God cares about you. Do not be deceived with negative images that tell you anything else.

❖ Your life is about you and your growth and development. As you grow and develop, do not forget to give back. It will continue to make you a better you.

CHAPTER 10

LEFT BUT NOT FORGOTTEN

MY NAME IS CAROLYN HAGEN. MY LIFE WAS A BLACK HOLE. I WAS EMPTY AND ALONE. I USED "58 POINTS TO SUCCESS AND TRANSFORMATION" TO CHANGE MY LIFE. HERE IS MY STORY...

CAROLYN HAGEN

At the age of 8 years old, I lost my mother to domestic violence. Her common-law husband had killed her. My self and three other siblings two brothers and one sister were placed with a family member an aunt, during my stay there I was raped by her son numerous times under her care.

One day my younger brother did something that my aunt was not pleased with and he was beaten with an extension cord , the next day he was sent to school and a school staff member noticed bruises and marks upon his body. The Department Of Family And Children took us from under the care of my Aunt and became our custodian parents we then became ward of the court until they decided where to place myself and my siblings. During this time me and my siblings was separated and placed in various foster homes.

I remember one foster home as if it was yesterday, in this home I was not allowed to eat the same meal as the family or sit at the dining room table with the family. One of the chores that were assigned to me was to assist her biological daughter with her homework, I didn't feel love or acceptance from this foster home I was placed in, it seemed as though I only existed. Then one day I was transferred out of that foster home to another foster home, where I was joined with my biological sister. Yes I was excited to finally be reunited with my biological sister , but I was also filled with a lot of pain, hurt, rejection, anger, resentment , brokenness and so many emotional problems that a child my age should not have experienced at such an age.

There I met a great woman of God by the name of Mrs. Jennie P. Hughes she was a phenomenal and God fearing woman she was also full of love and compassion. When she would discipline you she would always say " If I spare the rod I spoil the child" . She would state to all of the children as for me and my house we will serve the lord, this was not an option but a way of life. Every time the doors of the church was open , I found myself along with the other foster kids attending Sunday and morning service as well as evening service as a family. We all went together no one was allowed to stay home.

I was taught how to clean and do house chores and complete every chore that was given to me , I remember my first meal in this home Mama Hughes had prepared steak and everyone was seated at the table at the same time I said to her do I get to eat this ? she replied everyone in this house eats the same meal. Her love and compassion began a healing process in my life. Even though I tried to suppress and mask the darkness within me. Growing up in this house was the best thing that could ever happen to me. I learned how a home that allowed God to be in control produced **real fruits** that the bible speaks about which are long suffering , goodness, love, temperance just to name a few. What I experienced was genuine for Mama Hughes loved all her foster kids equally as if she had given birth to them herself. As I reflect back God had called and anointed Mama Hughes to be a foster parent. She was in this field of work for thirty plus years within this family all the children had to learn to live together with each other and work together with each other. Learn how to love and forgive each other, she showed no favoritism towards the children. She would discipline you and believe me I had my share of being disciplined and my behind being beat and she still displayed the love of Christ.

As a child I attended Liberty C. Elementary and went on to Filer Middle School and then went to Miami Northwestern Senior High, While between my eleventh and twelfth grade I was engaged to a young man who at the time was in the arm force (The Marine Corp) I was in process of preparing for my wedding to marry who I thought I would be spending the rest of my life with. Upon coming home from school one day , my mom stated to me the man who I was engaged to was already married to someone else. I don't remember after those words did I receive a letter in the mail from him that same day or the next day. But I do recall within two days I received a letter from him stating he had gotten married to someone else while I was preparing our wedding. Immediately I threw everything that I had bought for the wedding in the trash.

I blamed God, I felt like I had missed out on my husband because I was so involved in church activities and I said the next man that I get involved with I will spend all my time with him instead of being involved in the church like I were before. While still in high school I was trying to deal with the hurt, betrayal and pain, I then began to go down this spiral road of destruction. Looking and seeking for love and acceptance, I met a man whom I got involved with while trying to deal with my pain and hurt. I would constantly ask the question why men are like dogs. He replied "Men are no good" while in this relationship I became pregnant my second year of college. During the time of my pregnancy he provided for me an apartment and also paid all of the bills. Close to my ninth month of pregnancy my Mom told me to come back home and I continued to attend college and work. After I had given birth to my daughter the young man I was engaged to previously come to the hospital to see me and my daughter what a surprise.

After my release from the hospital, I went back to live with my foster mom (Mama Hughes) ,while I was there with my mom she showed me what a woman should do concerning her body after giving birth. She also showed me how to care for a newborn baby, I had made a decision to go back to my apartment, Mama Hughes stated I didn't have to leave, but I stated to her, that she raised us and taught us how to make it on our own. How to pray and trust God , I knew with the teaching and training that I received that I will survive . I was always intrigued at how strong of a woman that my Mom was with her gifting and talent's she truly was a Proverbs 31 woman.

She would tell her girls you may get married and you may not get married, but you will know how to keep a home and how to survive. It wasn't always easy but I never had to return back home. I had to experience life,(Mama Hughes) will tell me on various occasions that your Aunt wanted to know why I never called her. And that she would always receive a call from my sister. I responded to my Mom that I never heard her say anything good about my biological Mom. The words that would come out of Aunt mouth was negative Mama Hughes said you need to let her know how you feel .So one day my sister called our Aunt and asked me if I want to speak to her my first response was no, but I realized this was a away to clear the air and bring closure to this matter. I began to release all that was within my heart towards her and she stated I didn't know that I was the cause of our distance and she apologized for her actions.

Before my daughter reached the age of two years old her father was murdered. And when I attended the funeral service at the service I notice there where a lot of other women there that he had fathered children with also.

After graduation at Miami Dade College in 1979 I went to FIU a university to continue my education in social work. My daughter started having some health issues that took a toll on me trying to attend college and take her to various doctors she was scheduled to see. I had to drop out of college and continue to work and provide for my daughter.

During this time I met an older guy that I got involved with and within the fourth year of our relationship I became pregnant. The strange thing about this is that on one particular night of intimacy I heard the voice of the lord say you're pregnant I just blocked it out of my mind and didn't want to receive it. Eventually I told him I'm pregnant, he really wasn't ready to have any more children I told him that I'm not going to abort this child. And if I have to raise him/her alone so be it. He supported me thru out my pregnancy, when I delivered the child I didn't let him know about the birth of his son until after his birth. He was in his son life until we went our separate ways. When his son was between three and five years old I noticed he didn't seem to have time to spend with son because of the woman that he was involved with. He told me one day that this woman didn't mind him seeing his son as long as he didn't bring his son to his house that he owned.

One day I had a dream concerning him I told him that in this dream that he was sick and confine to a wheelchair. And he would look out his large living room window wondering why his children didn't come to see him within this dream this woman he was in relationship with would intercept his phone calls and when his children would come by his home she denied them access to him.

He proceeded to end that relationship and began to confess other things to me he then resumed a healthy relationship with his son. I was involved in relationship after relationship that continued to spiral down. One day Prophet Mary Grant whom I considered like a spiritual Mother that I had visited one day because she wasn't feeling well, began to tell me "Carolyn you have allowed so many things to come between you and God, men, flesh, your issues etc. I'd gotten so upset with what she had spoken to me, that I left her home and went walking six blocks back to my home. As I continued to walk, I kept hearing within my ears over and over the words that she had spoken.

As several days passed by, one day I sat down at my dining table and had a one on one with self. I began to look at my life and decided to be truthful with myself. I said to myself out loud Carolyn you have allowed men, flesh, issues, un- forgiveness, pain etc… to come between you and God. So I decided to make a change for the better. I told my male friend who was an Evangelist. That I'm not going to fornicate any more that I'm going to do it God's way. I really thought he would understand and except what I said I was shocked at his response "So now you want to be sanctimonious I began to tell him as long as I 'm giving you what you want but because I wanted change and to do what was right in God sight you now have a problem, I stated to him thank you very much. Cause the scales has come off my eyes.

I attended various ministries was dedicated and faithful committed to whatever I had to do in God's house I had experienced betrayal from five different leaders with in the gospel. I know what character assassination feels like, being lied on where people begin to look at you strange and make remarks I thought you were to look like ___ and I would say like what and people would change their conversation sowing accordingly to what the leader said from one hundred dollars to one thousand dollars for the kingdom to find that the Man Of God was supplying his woman not wife with lavish gifts. Using God money for self -gain instead of building the kingdom of God. As people was giving toward the vision of the house, when it came for my transition from a particular ministry to Greater Harvest Christian Church.

When I first laid eyes on Apostle Dr. JG Rice, I couldn't explain what I was experiencing on the inside I felt like a sponge soaking up what God was saying on to a dry sponge, being filled with the living spring of water (life) I knew that I needed what was within the Woman Of God prior to me being at my former Church I've spoken to the Pastor and she knew that I was there just for a season. I didn't know when my release would come or how it would come I started to attend Harvest University under Challenger Apostle Dr. JG Rice and Bishop James Rice.

I couldn't afford to miss any days my former Pastor and I

would attend regularly, then she begin to make excuses and say tell the Apostle this or say that to her God would have her call just before I would get on the express way to come pick her up. I would say, you told me you were not going she would say I just gotten off the phone with the Apostle.

I didn't feel right and I noticed a change with the Pastor and I knew what dripped from the head down to the beard, affect the body I needed to move and I needed a change for my life. Both leaders came together and I was received as the new member to be under Apostle and Bishop Rice. My former Pastor stated she was releasing me with good intention and blessing when in actuality she spread out venom towards, called me a liar, a hypocrite because I know what God was doing for me .She kept blowing up my phone leaving all kinds of ugly statements, I could not believe that a leader that I worked under would do such things. I let my leader Apostle Rice hear what was said and was told to delete it and don't allow it to get with in my spirit. One thing for sure if leaders are wounded they wound other leaders, especially when they are in denial.

Many times I stated to my former Pastor that she was operating within her flesh and she would say you're right and many times she would ask me my opinion and I would let her know when she was wrong and she stated to me " I didn't like what you said many times but I had to tell her the truth.

When I came to Greater Harvest I came as a woman who was torn, broken, not trusting leaders didn't want to get close or be close to any leader comfortable where I was in my flesh I Didn't want to do anything new I was stuck, in order to grow I had to be challenged in the things of God. Come out of complacency, being stretched doesn't feel good, learning that it's more to you than just a worshipper, pressing myself to be better. About Evangelism the importance of Evangelism is to stop being religious, being taught how to bring forth a message also the importance of a Webster dictionary, bible concordance, and a bible dictionary. Your three points and conclusions say what your leaders say according to the word. Wax on and wax off, how to pray the word, knowing where God is taking you people can't go. Expect jealousy get your mind right so that you can be positive in the right position.

I had excuses after excuses concerning why a project wasn't complete, cause I didn't want to deal with the drama of people. Here at the Greater Harvest my life has changed for the better, next I had to deal with the enemy within me and allow the work of God to change me from the inside out this has made me the woman – Preacher that God has called and chosen to be an (Kingdom Ambassador) for the kingdom of God. I'm grateful for the Apostle Dr. JG Rice a woman of Sternness a jewel in the kingdom of God, birthing forth sons and daughters on the structure and order of the kingdom of God how to operate within the kingdom.

Having integrity, allowing your Ministry to be proven and having the spirit of excellency. Because what you do for Christ will last.

Thank You Apostle Dr. JG Rice

CHAPTER 11

58 POINTS TO SUCCESS AND TRANSFORMATION

FACTORS 41 THROUGH 58

FINANCIAL EMPOWERMENT
FACTORS 41-55

Everyone wants it. To be RICH. To have money and wealth. And if you are a believer, you should. But if you get it, money that is, can you handle it?

Add up all the money you have made in the last 10 years and give an account for it. This will let you see if you are really ready to handle wealth.

You will probably need another sheet to be honest about your spending. But after you deduct as much as you can, see what you should be doing differently. It will help you with future resources!

Year	Amount	Where it was spent

Factor 41: "What's your Happy Goal?"

You need to discover your financial " Happy Goal." What amount of money will make you happy? What do you consider Financial Success?

Have a hot cup of coffee or tea and be real with yourself about how much money do you need monthly/ annually to be happy? Now process a plan to help you reach that goal.

First, get a business going for yourself. Your business. Your work. Your money!

Let's answer these questions:

I need _____amount of money per year to be happy.

I can start my own business and it will be:

_____

I will start my business on:

_____

Factor 42: Learn Monopoly

Yes, playing the game with someone else's money will give you a better feeling of managing your own. When you play Monopoly you will learn buying, trading and selling property. You will learn simple banking and real estate principles. Yes really, monopoly will help.

Factor 43: Know the Difference Between A Need and A Want

Love, clothes, food and shelter are the basic needs that must have priority of your spending habits. Things that fall outside of these categories must be evaluated to determine whether they are a need or a want. If you take care of your needs first, you will be well on your way to financial responsibility.

Factor 44: Invest in Wealth Training

Take classes at least two times per year. Plain and simple. You need to invest (spend Money) on your success. Often we go to a book store and buy books on the topic and read them. Other times we have to pay for courses to enhance our self and our financial empowerment, and so will you. Also, joining specific networking groups that address your business and the business you want to be in, is a good way to introduce yourself to others in the financial status you wish to gain.

Factor 45: Partnership are valuable

Don't try to do it all, in the beginning you will need help and training. If you have value you can trade "Value skills." For example, if you can type and you need some food for a special event… maybe a partner will fix some food for you if you design a new brochure for them. This is called "bartering" and will help you out a lot. That's why educational enhancements are a must. Otherwise you may bring no value to the table and will be paying for everything that you may need.

Factor 46: Time is VALUABLE

Invest precious time in others as long as they add value to your life. Stop hanging out with people who are not improving themselves financially. **Hanging around persons who have no interest in financial success will kill your dreams and visions of financial wealth**. Add new friends in business and new financial positions to your life, conversations, and social events. This will enhance your ability to continue to grow successfully.

Factor 47: Stop Playing– Get A Business

Everyone should own a business. Starting a business will give you 22 major business deductions You'll see why a business is a necessity for your future financial success.

Learn how to balance your check book and get a savings account. So when you need a business account, you have a relationship with a local bank, and they can help you start a new business account.

Factor 48: Get the Money—Honey

Meeting a "Human Need" will keep you in the " Cash Flow." Pick careers where people will always need your services and you will always have a career and cash flow.

Factor 49: Mentality of Ownership

Change your W-4. Manage your own money. Stop letting the Government manage it for you. What is a Tax Return? Your money coming back to you after you let someone else hold it and use it for a year! You lend the Government your money throughout the year, and they give it back at the end of the year... No interest.

Would your budget be different if you could add $200- $500 extra dollars to your budget a month? Would that help you to start a business? Well go for it! Change your W-2 today and give yourself the maximum deductions allowed now and use your own money for success. Pull that money now, and use it to start a Business. Start acting like a business owner, Invest in YOU!

Factor 50: Business is WORK

If you plan to invest in "Real Estate" learn about all the loans, including hard money loans. And all other facts. There are no "get rich quick" businesses, you must work. Work your business and the business will work for you. Don't spend your money if you think you will get rich within 90 days because it WILL NOT work.

Everyone selling the "I can make you rich" products are not telling you about the many hours you must work to make the business pay off. Do not look to get rich overnight. This is not sensible and will disappoint you in the long run. Plan to be in business and achieve success by hard work. Only constant hard work will cause you to succeed. No tricks, no gimmicks. Just hard honest work.

Factor 51: What is your "Why?"

Your why is "Why you do what you do." When you strive for financial success, you must make sure your "WHY" is big enough to push you into success.

WHY ...   am I in this business
WHY ...   do I do what I do
WHY ...   do I want to success

Factor 52: New Things are Coming

Make room for new things, throw away five old things and make room for new things.

1) Sell if you can
2) Donate if you can
3) Throw away things you don't need
4) Make room for increase

List 5 things you are going to rid yourself of to get new things:

1. _____

2. _____

3. _____

4. _____

5. _____

Factor 53: Learn the Tax Laws

No one is going to tell you how to save yourself thousands of dollars for free. You need to get to know the tax laws. Take a tax class and find out what deductions you may be able to get. These new tax laws will increase your inner growth, business growth, and you will be able to help your friends and family save money as well.

Factor 54: There's Plenty of Money

As we learned in the Election Process of 2008, billions of dollars have been spend on electing a candidate. There is no shortage of money. Think about it, where does the money come from? **PEOPLE!** These same people are available to you, if you bring them a plan they can buy into. Do you believe that someone will pay you for what you do or know? Well you'd better. The money is out there. Go get it!

Factor 55: Make it Right

Make your product in excellence ALL the time. Spend the time to do it right, and it will bring additional business to you. I teach Small Business Start-Up Classes, and at every class I give the new students the opportunity to present their business and talents. Of course I want to see EXCELLE NCE!

Recently one student wanted a catering business, so I gave her the opportunity to cater for the small class. No big to do I told her. To my surprise this student went all out, getting her catering dishes, spoons and napkins. The food was good, but the presentation made me want to immediately refer her to others needing a caterer.

You see, everyone is always watching to see if you are as

good as you say. Your efforts always represent you, so put out your best effort every time. You will be surprised to know who will recommend you, because of your excellence.

Factor 56: DO IT RIGHT THE FIRST TIME! It will save you money and time of re-doing it again.

Don't cheat yourself. Add cost before ever giving prices. And add staff cost. Then set your price to represent your services. You do not have to be the cheapest, if you are confident you will do the best job. Be fair with your ability to make and increase, then you nor your clients should be disappointed when you use these strategies.

SUMMARY

- ❖ You should really have a business. This is your new goal for the next 3-6 months, to plan to have a business.

- ❖ After deciding what this business should and will be, market your product professionally.

- ❖ **Junk will get a "junkie" price. Excellence gets a better price.** What does your product look like? Always strive to improve it, revise it and revisit it for your success.

- ❖ Truth creates money, lies destroy money. Be real to yourself.
- ❖ Look at what you have, not at what you have already used.

- ❖ Do what's right for you. It will create what is right for your money.

- ❖ Invest for Death. Plan to leave an inheritance to your grandchildren.

- ❖ Use your credit cards, but pay all charges off every two months. If you can't pay it off in two months don't use credit.

<u>LASTING POINTS FOR SUCCESS</u>
FACTORS 57

<u>Factor 57: "Always pay yourself!"</u>

Pay yourself at least 10% of your income

Give to Charity or invest in your Church at least 10% of your income.

Save 4% of your income for **Emergencies.**

Use 4% of your income each year for **vacations** and special events for yourself and with your family.

<u>The other 70% of your income should reach this value breakdown:</u>

50% **Living Cost & Expenses**

 6% other **Bills**

2% **Splurge** money

3% **Investments** (to make additional Money)

1% **Insurance & Health**

2% **Retirement Fund** (and don't forget to leave the government their part maximum)

7% **Taxes**

The Extra Penny…oh well, **buy an ice cream cone.**

Get a dollar worth of change and do this distribution so you can really see what and how your money should be handled. Or you can get $10 in ones and do the same percentage breakdown. It will really help you to try and start a new pattern for wealth development.

Factor 58: You are in CONTROL!

You are in control of your life (with the creator of course), and you have the responsibility to take control of your life. You have the power to do so with skills, understanding, creativity, choices, educational enrichment, supernatural energy and health, spiritual identity, and financial empowerment. Using these principals will create for you and your family **SUCCESS!**

FINAL SUMMARY

❖ Remember that your health and mindset are as important as your financial goals and business dreams. You must embrace the MINDSET of tithing, doing good, and paying back & forward. These thoughts will cause you to become a "financial current" and good things will always come back to you.

❖ Turn everything that's invaluable in your life into an asset or get rid of them. If it brings no value it must be done away with. De-clutter your life and see the good things God has already blessed you with.

❖ "Faith without works is dead." Take an active RESPONSIBILITY for your financial success. Set reasonable financial goals. Start the 71 day plan to retrain your mind, thoughts, life patterns, and business goals.

❖ You decide how much "wealth" is drawn to you. Join networking groups, social activity groups, and money groups to enrich your knowledge and make new business contacts.

❖ You must become healthy wealthy, and wise. Read new materials, enhance your skill levels, and seek positive environments. Purpose in your heart and mind to attract wealth.

CHAPTER

12

I WENT FROM BEING JUST DUMB TO CHURCH DUMB, NOW I'M FINALLY IN THE KINGDOM

MY NAME IS SHIRLEY MCINNIS. I WAS DROWNING IN FINANCIAL DEBITS AND IN DESPAIR. I USED APOSTLES BOOK "IT'S ALL ABOUT THE KINGDOM" AND FACTORS 41-58 TO TURN MY LIFE AND FINANCES AROUND HERES MY STORY....

SHIRLEY MCINNIS

I never really realized how dumb I really was/am until The Master Prophet herself (Chief Apostle Dr. J.G. Rice) called me in her office while service was going on. "I believe she picked up in her spirit that my mind was gone. I wasn't focus. Apostle is so sharp that in the spirit she can be Preaching, Singing, Praising all through service even Praying with her eyes close and still see from a far. (She doesn't miss too much of nothing) And in the mist of our conversation Apostle asks me one question, so what kind of grades did you get in school? Well I graduated with a 3.2, so I guess that wasn't so bad. Apostle said so I figured you was smart but YOU STUPID! She said don't get offended but YOU STUPID! "You don't have a teachable spirit" You're too smart to act so dumb; God has a purpose for you, grow up in the things of God. You're going to have to ask God to help you release something's, In order to get the fullness of God deliverance for you, you must go back to the root of it. "Where it all started"

Apostle said, "I need to you to get yourself together. I don't need to hear about your past because I already see your Future. God is going to use you; I need for you to start focusing on your Future. My Job is to get you to the next level.

At this point in my life I've never had a preacher or prophet or anyone that was bold enough to tell me the truth about me. I've been in and out of church for so long never to have any one to take a mirror and show me, me. Before I met the Chief Apostle Dr. J G Rice, I'd just recently relocated from Cleveland Ohio back to Florida living with at the time my boyfriend and family. I only returned to Florida because God was missing in my life. I wanted to come home from all the chaos I'd involve myself in Cleveland. The only reason I move to Cleveland Ohio is because I'd just got kick out of Atlanta Job Crops college program with a completion of graduating with a standard certificate in business administrations at the age of 24. I just couldn't return back to Florida without at least a degree in something. I knew when I left Florida; I'm determine to make something better of myself. (At least those were my plans) So Cleveland came to mind, made some phone calls to my past, contact some people that watched over me as family the couple of years when I'd lived there before, and now I'm off to Cleveland Ohio.

Where a new life was awaiting me there that I'd thought I could handle. I arrived there like little miss goodie too shoes. I didn't drink at the time "recovered alcoholic" delivered from smoking. I use to smoke so much in Florida growing up, until I starting thinking that I'm going to be a crackhead. But it didn't take long for me to start, drinking at least. Hanging around so many different spirits on everyday basics, I became that teen age girl that I'd run from in Florida. My teenage years were a mess and I wanted no parts of being that little girl anymore. I could remember when I told one of my older cousins that "my life is boring" and I needed some drama; and boy did I get exactly what I was looking for. Through the years adjusting to my new found home and family. I started working for this company with MRDD "mentally retarded disabled development" even worked my way up to team leader and supervisor. I went to Ohio school of Broadcasting and graduated. I had it going on, eventually I had my own place, most of the time living in Cleveland I had a car or some type of transportation.

I believe that out of all the spirits that I were dealing with on an everyday bases, "acceptance, rejection, depression, doubt and unbelief, emptiness, disappointment and loneliness. (And that's just to name a few) Somehow, with all these mixed emotions going on, I'd stop loving myself again. It's funny because I'd just learned how to really love myself before I left Florida to Atlanta Ga. for job crops. I'd learned that I didn't need a man to make it, that I am somebody through Christ Jesus who strengthens me. I really don't blame my surrounding, however it's only but so long you could fight your flesh from its desires. I still had stuff in me that I thought was dead. I allowed myself to be caught up in situations that cost me money, time and more money. For at least 3 to 4 years straight I'd found myself working to pay and keep a car; either I was dumb enough, to let somebody borrow my car or they'll tear it up. Or, some crazy knuckle head dude will tear it up for me, or I'd just wouldn't fix the car and eventually get another. Either way I went through more cars in my life in that time frame, from buying them to renting them. "I just had to drive" Honestly, I'd just went to sinking again, I became a flat out drunk, and nobody couldn't stop me. I was In and out of these relationships, hoping that somebody will love me enough to make me stop. God did bless me with a friend that truly loved me, he would do anything for me. "Him or his family" But I'd took advantage of his love, I couldn't no longer hide who I'd truly become. When I'd finally offered myself to him for sex, he didn't want me. He's the only man that didn't lower his love for me because of my body. He'd loved me beyond sex, and since I couldn't understand that he could be more than just my friend. "How I wished more men were like that" on the other hand, I used men and they'd used me for that ten minute connection. It was so bad, that this one young dude with nothing. I mean he had nothing, for nothing, with nothing, and about nothing. All he had were a bunch of children to show for his life of only 23, but I just had to have him. Not saying I couldn't do better, which I did, from drug dealers to barber shop owners, a bartender, business owners, property owners' a radio host, shade tree mechanics, bus drivers, a truck driver, I mean, most of the men had to at least provide me something. Especially in a need! But this young "beater eater"-that's my nickname for him, because that was all he was ever good for. Oh boy, did I lose my mind for him. He had the car, drop me off to work at one point, and gave him gas money. All he was good for is giving me an excuse for not wanting anything better for myself.

I've been Homeless on two different occasions in Cleveland Ohio. I've lived in a homeless shelter states, sold drugs in both states. "Nothing major.

This is just some of my Testimonies. Not to mention how the church use to always make an example out on with different demon and spirit until it became a show of entertainment.

I use to rob and Steal, break into people houses for what I thought was survival. I've had a couple of so call boyfriends to go across my head. I went across a head or too myself now.

So when Apostle told me I needed balance, you can see why now. "I can too" Chief Apostle Dr. J G Rice along with Arch Bishop James Rice are not the kind of people that want to hear a problem without a solution. They don't ask for problems they want the solutions; and one of my main issues is that I'm to focus on the Problem and not the solution.

Not too long after that talk with Apostle although I wasn't there at that low point in my mind anymore Apostle preached on don't be shaken in your Mind. So Now I use that word to War off the attacks of my Mind.

"Apostle doesn't cut any corners; she's the realest I've ever met, behind or in front of the pool pit." (And I'm Grateful for her) The best part of her being real is that she has "NO" respective Person. Meaning she don't care who you are, if it don't line up with the word of God, than it's out of order and you are too. The Apostle love to make this statement when peaching that "If I hit you than I didn't mean to miss you "Apostle is a true word believer and teacher. Not just because she has a whole lot of Scriptures in her, it's because she's living it. Chief Apostle Dr. J G Rice is the first person to ask a question; what is your purpose? That she purposely wake up on purpose. "I didn't understand it at first, but through the word of God, I understand more and more now. Some may think how a person can wake up on purpose when you really don't know if you're going to wake up. But Apostle is teaching me that only what you do for God will last. And until you truly Know who you are in Christ Jesus/ or as Apostle like to say is when you're rested in God. That's when you're Faith that rested on grace and mercy speaks to you and says, "I have a kingdom assignment to fulfill". There's more work to be done in the kingdom, it's all about the kingdom for the body of Christ. Apostle truly understands that you better work while its day, because when night cometh no man shall work. And she demands that from me. Apostle truly carries the mantle of a priest of the Old Testament due to she's not going to accept a blemish offering. "A Powerful Woman of God": A Woman of Excellence.

Most Pastors or preachers even some prophets, the most they ever saw in me was money, miracles or a demon. That's when I was truly in being church dumb. But to keep it real, when she said how stupid I really was. I couldn't argue. I allowed myself to be taken to places in my mind from my past that the enemy begins to use to bring doubt and unbelief. I was shaken in my mind. On most Fridays night doing service Apostle allow testimony times. I always wanted to tell my story, tell how God brought me out from being so dumb. But I was afraid until now.

Going back to when Apostle sat me down in her office and told me off about me, I didn't get offended. (Not to say I haven't or will "Praise the Lord" But I understand that if I do, It's my flesh and it must die; and I'm not going up against the Apostle but the spirit of God that's in her. "And I know God is with her so my Prayer is to God to change me. Apostle has been saved, Preaching and Teaching before I was even thought of. So I know it's me. Just like the Arch Bishop says, Shut up! "You just got here". "So I do my best to Shut Up", and try and learn something because I truly just got here, not knowing anything. The Chief Apostle was right, I had go way back to the root of it so I can allow God to heal my wounded areas in my Life and take away the tricks of the enemy.

The Roots of me made me ashamed of me all my life. "Real Talk" But thank God he had a plan for me even in the womb; because the enemy tried to take me out even as an infant. The rumor was that after birth I had some type of complications. Although, I was born in a town that's called Clewiston in Florida: I was rushed to Miami Children hospital where I stayed until up to almost 6 to 8 months. And it was said that that the elderly woman from 68 to 70 years old "Mary Lou Bernard"(who was a praying woman of God) would have another praying woman to take her to Miami from a small town of Belle Glade to Pray for me every week until I was made whole. In other words God had to send the real mothers of the church on my behave. That knew how to stir something's up in the atmosphere: Thank you Jesus.

Defeating My Greatest Enemy; The Demon in Me

Now I've been attack by the enemy all my Life. As I grew older I could remember reading up on having a imaginary friend and in most cases the child has to have had a traumatic experience; where that child uses there figment of their imagination to create a character for comfort, for safety, even for blockage reasons. Now that I look back my imaginary friend was develop out of all the reason or excuses.

That's another reason I am so grateful for the Apostle Dr. J. G. Rice. She has that old time praying anointing of the real church mother's. You know the ones that will make you get on your knees and have to call on Jesus, Jesus, Jesus, Jesus, Jesus, Jesus, Jesus. Call on Jesus until something moves, until he answers, until you come up to another level: And if that's all you got than use it, do something to reach the power of God. The Apostle teaches firmly in you have to grow in God; and if it's not growing then it's Dead.

As I got older trying to reclaim my walk with God, even when the desires of me having children hunted me. I always felt that the reason why I couldn't have any children is because of what I did to the children from my past in as a child.

While attending our annual WOMAN conference on August 24, 2013 (I do realize that I'd use the word woman instead of women because I'd learned the difference between Female and Woman. Although I'd already the meaning Woman but to understand the spiritual aspect of it was an eye opener; and besides if she wasn't talking to anyone else she was talking to me. So Apostle had one of her very good friends come and speak for us; the entire minister had a real word from God but this speaker took it to another level about letting go some of my past hurts and pains that have kept me in bondage for so long. And she'd taken off her shirt with another shirt under it with holes and words like RAPE, BETRAYAL, MOLESTED, LOSS CONTROLL, ANGER, FEAR, LIED ON and she wanted me to write all that applied to us on sheet of paper all that applied and own it.

Because it's easy to say you forgive someone but she explained the power of pardon. And she thought us how to pardon every individual that may have cause this bondage from our past. The Arch Bishop Rice had been teaching that when a traumatic experience occurs that a emotion is tired up with it and basically he was teaching about controlling those emotions. Or, like Apostle would say guard Your Heart)

So the minister also wanted everyone to write down every person name down to that may have caused this bondage. And then she'd begin to call us up one by and when she ask me is all of this is your pain and hurts. I smiled and said yes. Then she asks me did, I own It? Wow, unlike most of the other women there I added others word such an ABONDONMENT ISSUES because that's what I had. I could remember the Apostle talking to me and out no where she'd stated that I want leave you; and when she said it, it kind of took me for loop. Like why would you say that? Apostle always has a way addressing your spirit man. I had to write down some stuff I really didn't want to face. Not only did someone hurt me but I've hurt others and I needed God to release some things in me as an OPRESSOR, I had some people that I needed to forgive but I had to write down some people names to ask God to soften that person's heart so they can forgive me. Then she'd stapled the paper with me.

After the minister close, Apostle always has to bring clarifying anything that was let unexplained. So the apostle begins to explain on how that was something I did but I don't have to own it because doesn't define me now. That's your past, not who you are now.

When Apostle said that I took the staple off with the paper: before apostle spoke bishop just added to our conference that God declared War against the Woman and the serpent. And Apostle began to encourage and prophecy in my Life I don't have to except that. The Apostle along with Bishop is training me to how to overcome all obstacles just by going through. How to really live Save and sanctified filled with the Holy Ghost. How to decree and declare some things; and truly stand on the word of God. To go to Glory to Glory; their prime examples of a True Faith walk. Apostle is truly is Woman of God that full of a Faith. If she loses everything else oh God don't take her Faith. I never had seen a Woman that has so much on all things and matters. Until when she walk into any store everything just went on sale. Because if the price don't match the money she's expecting to pay than Gods moves it to her standards.

God said in his word that Apostle came to set the captive free. To open the prison doors. So I'm no longer in bondage in my mind I've been made free. Although there's more to my story, whether I tell it or not it's finally just a story so others can hear How the power of God still works. Do not matter how long you've been trap in your circumstances. God is truly a way maker, He's truly a Deliver, When I could've lost my mind completely he set in and anointed me and told the devil you can play with her but don't take her mind. "The book of Job taught me that the devil has to get permission to do anything to you" But I thank God that I have a real covering some leaders that is going to tell me that's not God. A Leader that truly watches for my will mind and Emotions and is always on watch. "Thank you Jesus" When I first started out at Greater Harvest Christian Center Churches Worldwide (one church in 12 locations) I was broken, wanted to give up. Just go on living and give on the promise God had given me. God had sent me to a place that I'd long desire for and restore every promise back into my mind and Heart. Made me Free; Showed me the vision; Made pick it up and understand that their training me to become Solider in the army of the Lord; and I can't go through life shaken without no power; A Solider without any bullets. "As Apostle would say" So just like Bishop taught me that, I have to make a decision. Bishop James Rice is the first person to believe in my dream of being a pilot. He's always encouraging me not to let go of my dream. That's just what I'm doing; I don't care how I feel anymore! What it may look like! Are even if I do get offended.., I will not be shaken or moved from my position from my leadership privilege. I mean there's no place like the Greater Harvest Christian Center Churches Worldwide.

No longer will I allow myself to be just stuck on Stupid in the things of God or in the world. I am a Kingdom citizen and I want come off the wall.

CHAPTER 13

"GRACE VS. GHETTO"

REALIZING THAT GOD WANTS TO TAKE
US OUT OF THE GHETTO AND INTO GRACE
IN OUR MINDS

It's in the Book!

I am coming from the book of Philemon. Philemon is a one chapter book that a person may wonder, "Why would he even include this? What's so powerful within this one chapter?" Paul wrote this to the Philemonites:

"Paul, a prisoner of Jesus Christ, and Timothy our brother, unto Philemon our dearly beloved and fellow laborer" (Philemon 1:1)

So here we find that Paul is actually writing to a person. And that the person, the Philemonite, name is Philemon.

"And to our beloved Apphia and Archippus our fellow soldier and to the church in thy house." (Philemon 1:2)

So what did we learn right there? That there was not always these big Ephesus. **Everybody is not called to a big Ephesus.** There are churches that have been born out of houses, out of living rooms, out of bible studies, out of barber shop meetings, out of back porch meetings. So here Paul is talking to the overseers, Apphia and Archippus, the fellow soldiers, and to the church that's in their house. They actually had a church in the house!

When God gives you a place of residence sometimes it's not always about you. It's about bringing the glory into where you are. You may stay in an area where the people can't get to your church. But you know what? You should have two or three friends that you can invite over and say, "You know what? Let's go over what I learned in bible study. Let's have a little prayer and play my Apostles CD. Let's play the Bishops CD. Let's pray the Word of God. Let's create a Youth Ministry or a Ladies Group." Bring the Glory of God to your area.

God the Father, Jesus the Son and the Holy Spirit

Paul says,

"Grace to you, and peace, from God our Father and the Lord Jesus Christ." (Philemon 1:3)

Now again, Paul is separating God as the Father and Jesus Christ as Lord. I tell people this all the time. I say, "Listen, if God and Jesus were one, when Jesus died that means God would have died." God has never died. His only begotten son died and was hung on the cross. God never went to the grave. He has never died. And if Jesus and God was the same exact person, when he was talking to his Father and said,

"Father unto thy hand I commend my spirit." (Luke 23:46)

He would have been schizophrenic because he would have been talking to himself. **Jesus is not schizophrenic**. There's the Father, the Son and the Holy Ghost.

When Jesus says me and my Father are one, it's almost like… you see Jayden and you see Will Smith. You may say, "Boy, you look just like your daddy." And if you're driving at night in tinted windows and Jayden is driving his daddy's car you might say that that was Will Smith. They both share the same DNA, but they are two different entities, even though they are in the same bloodline. Now can Jayden take his daddy's driver's license and go cash his daddy's check? Yes, if the teller doesn't look real close. She will give him his daddy's inheritance. But if it comes time to serving time in jail, somebody's going to stand up and say, "That wasn't me!" So when he says here,

"I only do what my Father says do." (John 5:19)

"I only speak what my Father says to speak." (John 12:50)

"When you see the Father you see me." (John 14:9)

It's like Jayden saying, **"If you want to know what my daddy looks, when you see me, you see him."** He's not saying I am him. When Jesus said,

"I go to prepare a place for you." (John 14:2)

He went, he's gone. Jesus is not on this earth. He says,

"But I will leave you a comforter called the Holy Spirit, and he will live and abide in you."(John 14:26)

I see dead people!

So when people say, "I saw Jesus, I saw God." No, you saw a familiar spirit and that image is the only image you know so you attach that to seeing God. But be careful when you say spirits visit you. Any spirit that rests in you, doesn't visit you. It's a familiar spirit, which you need to cast away from you. We have no dealings with the dead. The Bible says we don't have any dealings with the dead. People that go and conjure up people to talk to them and deal with the dead. That's witchcraft. Talking about their mothers spirit came to them. No, that was a familiar spirit in the form of your mother, in the form of your father, or in the form of your uncle. Because either your mother is in heaven or hell, and that spirit you saw came to start a demonic work in your life. And so you have to cast those things away. That's why you shouldn't be calling up folks, playing with the Ouija Board, turning over tarot cards. All that is of a demonic entity.

One God with many different names

Jesus was not speaking demonically when He was saying me and my Father are one, because that would mean two personalities. That would mean a bipolar-ism or a schizophrenic-ism is going on. That would mean there would be an outer body experience and He would be taking on the persona of God. **But there is only One God. One Faith. One Baptism.** That's what the bible says. There's only one God.

Now people call him different things, but there's only one God. That's why you should never be thinking about leaving Christianity to move to another religion just because you call him Allah. Or you call him Jehovah. That's still His name. I am a Jehovah Witness. (Let me straighten that out because somebody got confused that I practice that faith or that religious belief.) I am a witness of Jehovah. I am definitely the Church of the Latter-Day Saints, because we are the saints of these latter days. I am definitely Baptist, because I've been baptized. I'm definitely Pentecostal, because I speak in tongues. I'm definitely Apostolic, because I believe in order. I'm definitely charismatic, because I'm not dead. Do you understand me now? So you can't get stretched and pulled away with people and the little things that they try to make so different from where you are. Because if you really know who you are, then you know there's only one God, one Lord, one faith and one baptism. Only one.

You cannot be caught up because people will always try to take what they think they know, and try to make what you think you know, of null effect. Can I help you? **Most people don't have the real Holy Ghost.** They have a ghost, but it isn't holy. How do I know? Because they have no keeping power and they have no changing power.

But... you're a woman

I had a person, oh this has been 15-20 years ago, that accosted me. I was at a garage sale, a yard sale, and the person accosted me because somebody came up and said "Hey Pastor, how are you doing?" I said, "Baby I'm doing fine, how are you doing?" [The person said], "Pastor? You're a woman Pastor? You're a Jezebel."

I said, "See you don't understand the spirit of Jezebel. Jezebel is not about a gender. It's about somebody that tries to push down the prophetic order and the word, the true word of the prophet, and won't let the true word of the prophet be told. Now why would you say I'm a Jezebel, you don't even know me? Why would you say I'm going to hell for preaching the gospel? Do you really believe God is going to send anybody to hell for telling somebody that you must believe in my son and be born again? He told all of us to go unto the edges and highways and compel people to come. How are you going to compel them if you aren't preaching the gospel? If He says, your sons and your daughters are going to prophesize. A prophetic word is going to tell you about your future. How am I going to tell you about your future if I haven't been touched with God today to tell me where you're going tomorrow?"

Now what's the difference if I tell it on the street corner or if I build a 2x4 and put a covering over your head and invite you in to hear it? If it's a starving sheep and they are being fed, God is going to send somebody to hell for feeding the sheep? God said,

"Beloved feed my sheep, feed my lambs." (John 21:15-17)

You can't let people twist your mind. **Because if I'm going to hell for preaching the gospel, certainly that's what you're going for too.** Obviously you're going to have a seat right by me. Because if preaching the gospel is going to get me condemn, then you might as well just turn over the book and close it because you aren't even going to make it.

A woman can't do that. The Bible said so.

So we can't condemn a person because there was a platform. This podium is made of wood. This'll burn up. This building will burn down. The gospels is still in me. And if I can tell you something that's going to help you change so you can have the power of God, God isn't going to condemn anybody for that. Gender doesn't matter. Gender is a thing that we have put limitations on. **"Well they said in Genesis that the man is going to have rule over the woman."** Well it also says in Genesis that you're going to sweat by your brow. It says your labor is going to be hard. If we are going to go to Genesis and we are both going to be under the curse. I'm not going to go out and work.

But Paul says,

"I wish a woman would keep silent in the church." (1 Corinthians 14:34-35)

The separation began when we first started coming into the temple. Men came in first and women were way in the back. And because of the Islamic rule you didn't talk to another man that was not your husband or family member. So when the Pastor was preaching and Deacon So-and-So wife wanted to know something, she would have to holler from the back and say, "What did he say? I don't understand that, explain that to me." So you have a hundred women hollering out "I don't understand. What did he say Todd? Tell me what he said, honey what's he saying?" **So Paul said, for order in the church, I wish that you all would keep silent and ask your husband's when you get home.** And if it meant that for everybody then what happened if you don't have a husband to ask when you get home?

So you have to understand the content in which it was said. And I tell people all the time, if you really want the women to keep silent, which means don't say anything, then why do you have them on your choir? Money answers all things, so why we paying money? Don't free me in one area and try to hold me hostage in another. The bible says that we are no longer under the curse. You're no longer under the curse. **I'm no longer under the curse. We went back to the original plan of God, which was to walk**

in equal dominion. Equal dominion. Equal dominion. Equal dominion.

We are ONE!

Let me give you an example. So God grows up a man named Michael in his own world, with his own family values and structure. And God grows up a woman named Mariah with her own family values and structure. Then one day these two meet. Michael was thinking before he met Mariah. But Mariah was also thinking. Her brain was moving, functioning and on track before she met Michael. You follow me? So then God pulls them together, and He says this is a mystery, how the two become one. Alright? Now, when we say Michael is quote on quote the head, Michael can't be the head any longer without Mariah because they two are one. So God begins to blend their minds together, their hearts together, their walk in life together. This makes a unity of one. The right side of the brain and the left side of the brain. The right eye, the left eye, the right lung, the left lung, the right kidney, the left kidney, the right leg, the left leg and one heartbeat. So now **the head cannot say I have no need of the eye, because my eye is your eye.** And the two became one. So what does he look like saying I am the head? The head of what? We both are the head. We both are the arms. We both are the foot. I can't operate one armed. We are one. We have to work TOGETHER!

What the world wants you to think is that when Mariah came to Michael she stopped thinking, love blinded her and she could no longer function. He's just supposed to be running things. She doesn't have a brain anymore. It's all about what he thinks. God would not subvert her like that. God would not put her in bondage like that. Because God loves her just like God loves him. And before he came in her life she was a living breathing thinking human. So there is no, you do what I say, Lording over her. Because when you Lord over somebody you miss the benefit of what they have to offer. And God wants equal dominion.

Relationship TRUST

God wants us all to know that He is rewards them that diligently seek Him. So when we diligently seek Him, we're seeking God for the best in life. We're not seeking for God to have anybody that will oppress us. Push us down. **But if you take what God taught me, and I take what God taught you, and we put it together and we walk as one, we can then conquer and defeat every demon.** Relationship trust comes in when you are not only like this (face to face), but you can turn around and be like this (back to back). Understanding that I conquer every demon from this side and I have your back. And you trust in the strength in me. And he's (my husband Bishop) is conquering every demon from that side. Therefore we have a 360 victory. Because I'm going to see some stuff that he isn't seeing, cause he isn't this way. And he's going to see some stuff that I'm not seeing. But yet we can communicate with each other and say, "Guess what baby, it's a bomb coming this way, lets both duck. Duck!" Say it with me, **"Victory!"**

I don't know how I got on this from Philemon. But am I helping you? Let's continue. It says here,

"Grace to you, and peace, from God our Father and the Lord Jesus Christ." (Philemon 1:3)

Grace and Peace

God wants us to have grace and peace. Grace is unmerited favor. When God told me I'm giving you grace, and I talk about this in my book "It's All About the Kingdom", I'm like, "Woo, another level in the Holy Ghost." He said no, I'm giving you grace, **I'm changing you name to Grace.** I'm like, "Huh, I already have grace, amazing grace." He said no, I'm giving you grace. He said you have class, but you don't have grace. The definition of grace is *elegance, beauty and form, manners, motions and actions. Pleasing and attractive qualities An endowment.* God said I'm giving you elegance, beauty and form. I'm giving you manners. I'm giving you motions and actions. I am giving you pleasing and attractive qualities. An endowment is a trust fund that has been set for you that at a certain age you receive it regardless to circumstance. So I was endowed with the power of grace.

It's raining FAVOR!

God gave me favor. That's why when I go into the store the blue light special come on. I operate under the anointing of grace. People think grace only has to do with salvation and that I sinned and that He gave me some grace, some mercy and grace. But grace has to do with your everyday life, your personality, how you carry yourself. It's a manifestation of favor. I'm not just talking about favor. I have uncommon favor!

See some people say, "How you doing? I'm blessed and highly favored." And I say, "Well how are you favored? What favor has been bestowed upon you today? What was your uncommon level today?" Yes, God woke you up this morning, but a lot of people woke up. What was your uncommon favor today? **What was your uncommon, unmerited favor today?** Something you didn't earn. Now if you walked up to a person they said its 20 something dollars for an item and you say, well what can you do to adjust that price? And they bring it down to $10.50 for you, that's Uncommon Favor.

When your superior, somebody that's over you or somebody that's in charge of something, can offer you unmerited favor. That means promotions. That means when everybody else is getting laid off and their hours are getting cut, your hours get extended. When they say there's no more hiring and I'm laying off everybody on the floor you already know, well I'm the one that isn't going home. I used to tell people when I didn't fly, I'd say, "If I did fly and the plane went down, I'd be the only one who'd survive." If only one person survive, it would be me to tell the story. I just believe like that. I believe in the uncommon and unmerited favor of God. Because he said to me I am giving you the gift of grace.

Some things God is going to give you is not tangible. Something's God is going to give you and speak to your life you will never understand it until 5-6 years later down the road. It's then that you will understand that the gift He gave you is awesome. The gift He gave you is spectacular! The gift He gave you money cannot buy it! You can't buy grace, God has to give you grace. God gave me mercy. That means when justice should step in, mercy has its way.

Class is in season

Sometimes God has to tell you what the difference is in what you think you have and who you really are. Now let's look at the word class. God tells me, you never had grace you have class.

Class   is
...a number of persons or things regarded as forming a group by re ason of common attributes, characteristics, qualities, or traits. See I was in a group. I had been instructed. I understood how to do things because of the instruction, but not because of the grace. I had my preacher group, I had my women's group, I had my Joshua generation group, I had my Judah group, I had groups. So groups determine class. By my attributes, my characteristics. The way I said, I'm not going to be known as a female preacher that someone can step up and say I slept with this woman. I'm not going to be known, tagged on the university, as the college campus hoochie. I'm not going to be known as somebody that's playing with God." **So I had set certain things in my character.** Certain things that I

said I'm not going to do this, God be my help. I'm not going to act like this, God be my help. So I had class. Qualities or traits that come forth. What are your qualities in your life? What are the traits in your life? That's your class. That sounds a whole lot different than grace. See I didn't understand the difference, God had to tell me. You don't have grace daughter, you have class. Now class isn't a bad thing, but grace is a whole lot better.

Now let's look up ghetto, because some of you don't have class because you have the ghetto. You're ghetto fabulous. You don't even get the traits necessary to have class. You don't even get the traits necessary to have grace. And see sometimes God has to speak to you and say this is the way you are, and you have to say, "Yeah, that is me." When I saw class I was like, "That is me." He said, "But now look up grace, that's what you're going to be." In one of the descriptions it also says a regal air of royalty, for grace. That's why they say Lady Grace. Her grace, when they refer to a queen.

Ghetto Fabulous?

Ghetto is *a section of a city, especially a thickly populated slum area, inhabited predominately by members of an ethnic or minority group, often as a result of social or economical restrictions, pressures or hardships.* You live in a radius of people that have economic and social hardships. **They have pressures and restrictions!** Did you hear the word restriction in class or in grace? It's only in the ghetto that restrictions apply.

A winter time is a restricted time. **When you have a ghetto mentality you have a restricted mentality.** It's not so much where you live, because if your mind set is not restricted you're not going to want to stay there. That's why some of you stay in sin because you're restricted to liking it. So you hang around with people that curse and have low social statuses and stay caught in the same rat trap. You won't go read a book to help bring you out of your ghetto-ness or your ratism, into another social dimension. That's why I love the show "House Hunters International" because they take me places that I might not get to go financially. I can go to Spain. Last night I went to Barcelona, and I went to Italy and I went to a place in Australia. Where did you go? And I looked at the houses. And I saw the houses they went in. I saw the lakes and the streets. Because if that's somewhere I want to go I need to get a picture. You will never come out of the ghetto until you change the picture in your mind.

Life in the ghetto

You expect certain things in the ghetto that you don't expect in a gated community. There are no bars in the community I live in, other than the gates that we come in. But yet there are a 1,000 people out there. If you go to Miami and you go to a 1,000 houses, 999 are going to have bars on the windows, bars on the doors and a big wolf dog out on in the yard. Why? Because **they are expecting to be robbed**. They have an expectation of someone coming on their premises to do something to them that they don't want done. We don't always lock our doors where we live because I don't have an expectation of anybody walking up in here and taking anything.

I'm the Moses!

I don't care if my family was raised in the ghetto. I'm the Moses. Did you get that? I'm the Moses. Somebody is going to put me in a basket and send me up the river for something better. I'm Moses. I'm not going to sit in the same despair. I'm Moses. I come to be a deliverer. I didn't come to be delivered. That's when you have to know the difference in the ghetto is that the ghetto needs to be delivered. There not the deliverer. **People with class come to deliver people out of the ghetto. People with grace come to get**

people with class from the people from the ghetto. So if nobody has grace in your life to be able to speak that level of deliverance to you so that you can come up even from you class, or from your ghetto mentality to class, you're going to stay in your social climate. That's why when I first started talking certain things to you it's hard for you to first click and receive because you've been ghettorized so long.

Fresh fruits taste the sweetest

You're not used to eating a fresh pineapple. You are used to the processed canned stuff that's up in the pantry. You have never chopped the top off a pineapple, even though you walk by them in the grocery store. Because you don't watch cooking shows that tells you how to go pick the pineapple and skin it down the side and cut it and chop it. Once you eat the pineapple and it get down it gets sweet. You won't want anything but fresh pineapples. You won't want anything but a fresh cantaloupe. You won't want anything but a sweet watermelon.

The Ghetto Mentality

Can I talk to you about the ghetto mentality for minute? Ghetto people go to the party and don't bring anything, but take 5 covered plates away. Even though somebody says to you, "Would you like to take a plate?," you don't go get 5 plates. You're ghetto! You have no class. You're acting like God isn't going to feed you tomorrow. Especially when you didn't bring anything. Class tells you to say, "No thank you, it's okay." And even if they bring you something you say, "Thank you very much, that's enough, please don't bring anything else." You could be hungry until your ribs go to your back, but the class in you....

Class is not just because you can dress up, but how do you act when you get dressed. Class is not going to let you wear something you can ball up in the palm of your hands out into public, because that's bedroom attire. If you can take your pants and ball it up in your hand, they aren't fit for you to wear outside. You don't have any class. You're ghetto! There are certain clothes they sell in the ghetto stores. You can go to certain areas and the clothing that they will sell you is cheap, there's no quality, it's all clingy, it's all revealing, because they feel like their dressing tramps and hookers. They put them outside on the little stand where you could see just how tight they are going to be on you. And you know you wear a 4x trying to get into an extra large. No, no, a medium, because you don't have any class yet.

Ghetto people will park the car outside the yard that hasn't ran for 4 years because they aren't even smart enough to call the people and get $600 for the junk car and use that for a down payment to go get another car. Are you ghetto? Ghetto people have parties that everybody in the neighborhood knows you got it. They don't have them in their house. They have to bring them all out in the yard, beer cans, cars up and down, loud people sitting on them carrying on and now there's a fight. Somebody got cut, now everybody runs to the fight so you can get shot. There are ghetto families where the whole family acts like banshees. Every month somebody is going to be fighting, because they don't have any class. They are in the ghetto, mentally. Ghetto people get food stamps on the 1st and don't have any food in their own house on the 10th.

Ghetto people get a bank account that starts you off with $50 and go take that money out and then close the bank account. Ghetto! Ghetto people put weave in their hair and dress up, but their children nose are snotty and their socks are dirty. Are **you living in the ghetto?** Ghetto people show up to your house with their 5 children and then disappear. They didn't feed them before they came and the kids are crying their hungry. But baby you're momma gets food stamps, didn't she feed you? "I'm hungry." You just got here 5 minutes ago, didn't you have breakfast? "I'm hungry." Okay your momma is ghetto.

Ghetto mothers show up to the school with their hair rollers, flip flops, those pants that I told you about that can be balled up in their hands, and get all in the teachers face talking trash. "Why you give my child a F? Why you give my child a F? You so stupid, you give my child a F. I don't like you no way. Stupid school." Baby, your child hasn't turned in any homework all year long, so yes your baby EARNED an F. Ghetto parents don't go to PTA or PTO. Why? Because they sitting on the front porch drinking 40s. "Momma PTA meeting is tonight. You better get in there and shut up, ain't no body going to the stupid school for you." Don't be ghetto!

Ghetto parents never volunteer at the school but they always have something to say. Ghetto people never have insurance on their car. You aren't classy driving around bumping into my car trying to hurry up and back up and leave because you don't have any insurance. We have more dings in our cars then we ever had down here in Florida And then the people just leave. They just hit your car and they just leave. You don't have any car insurance, but you're always at McDonalds. Don't you recognize that that same $10 you spend in a day on foolishness adds up to $300 a month and your insurance probably isn't anything but $150 or $125. So you can afford to do right, but you have to change your mind set. More than likely your momma didn't have any insurance. Yeah, I said your momma. You momma didn't have any car insurance either. And so because your momma didn't have any car insurance when you got your car, you momma didn't say, "You better get some insurance on that car." You're buying a car, but can you afford the gas, the insurance, and the maintenance? Cause momma doesn't fix any cars. And that happens within a radius of people.

What you have to do is get out of the radius. Change your location. **When you change your location, you change your mind set.**

In the ghetto there's always somebody walking the streets. Where I live there's nobody walking the streets after 10:30 pm, unless their walking the dog for a short pee and walking back in. But in the hood people stand on the corner until 4-5 o'clock in the morning. Don't act like don't know what I'm talking about. Some of them are your friends, your uncles, or your cousins but don't want to talk about them. On the corner 3 o'clock in the morning. Sleep 'til 11 o'clock in the morning. **In the ghetto you're not encouraged to finish school, education is not important.** How many times you've been to jail is important. How many people you shot is important. But when you move in the realms of class act and grace your mind set is going to change.

And so Paul says in the 3rd verse,

"Grace and peace from God our father and the Lord Jesus Christ. I thank our father for making mention of thee always in my prayer." (Philemon 1:3-4)

<u>Why are you screaming?</u>

So this is an intercessor. He says I make mention of you all the time in my prayer. I'm interceding for you to have grace and peace. Normally where ghetto follows there's no peace. When grace and class follows a situation there's going to be peace. You know you can tell somebody off without getting loud? Loudness is a sign of your ghetto-ism. Just because you got loud didn't mean something happened. So because you screaming like a banshee, hollering at the top of your voice, rolling your eyes, popping you neck like a chicken, and you didn't say at all. Just because you get loud doesn't mean you were right. Ghetto-ism makes you get loud. You can't even have a reasonable conversation. Nobody can sit you down and just talk it out. You're just ghetto, you aren't even fabulous. You aren't even bedazzled. You're just ghetto. You have no class. You have no grace.

Get out of the Ghetto. Get out of Egypt.

Change you state of mind

So you bring all those traits in anytime the pressure gets on you, and you fall right back into your ghetto-ism. So we can bring you out of the ghetto, but can we bring the ghetto out of you? **We can bring you out of Egypt, but can we bring Egypt out of you?** Are you always going to have to have somebody there beating you to make you do right? In the ghetto women love the men to beat them. "He loves me, see my eye. He love me, it's going to be alright Wednesday." You are so ghetto. "My momma was beat, you know me and her go with the same boy. He beat her, he beat me. It's my uncle though, you know." (Don't be shaking your head like you haven't heard the stories.) The uncle is the auntie boyfriend, the momma boyfriend, and you trying to get him. Everybody got a baby by him. All ya'll cousins is the same. Ghetto!

A ghetto woman wants her friends man. Women let me tell you something, when it comes to my Bishop, I don't play. See I know there are some half saved women in the church. They'll wear their skirt up to their navel and cross their leg and hope he looks. I'll wrap you up in a sheet and put you out the door. Because you're ghetto! **You have to protect what belongs to you. You have to protect your husband's eyes.** I don't even let my husband look at naked women on TV. I cover his eyes. Praise the Lord! "That's a spirit baby, cover up your eyes. She's a ghetto tramp, don't be looking at that ghetto tramp. You got class sitting right here by you, you got grace." Hallelujah!

And men, you all just look at these girls. You need to start saying, "That's stank ghetto."Because that girl will give you something you can't get rid of. Give you something makes you go bald before you get 30. Hallelujah! Make your hair fall out and itch. Praise the Lord! "Oooo she looks good!" No, she looks stank. You don't even know what looks good. **You've been so commercialized by tramps and tricks.** America is the only country that tricks and tramps can walk the streets. Any other country they say our women look awful. That they have no class. Because you figure because you show somebody everything you got, and that's what happens when you wear that spandex, but they don't want to buy it. So get your $2 and go home.

Women will sit in the church and pray your marriage dissolves so they can have your man. That's why women you better have the spirit of discernment when it comes to your men. **Have a spirit of discernment when it comes to your man.** Know that you aren't the only woman in life that he's going to be attracted to. And learn how to step in between that attraction and say it's about to be a fatal attraction up in here. Hallelujah! Because sometimes it's not about sex, it's about power and control. It's about can I sneak and do it. Can I get away with it? Women, same thing. Don't let your eyes fool you when those biceps and triceps walk by. When the 6 pack and 2 packs and cartons, some of them have cartons, got them lined up, walk by. You got to know that's a tramp. He just a male tramp. I'm happy at home. I'm well taken care of. I'm blessed to have a man of God. I wouldn't trade my man of God in for nothing, because we are one. And grace and peace is upon our relationship. And so when you look for somebody, don't look for somebody you can trick with a tramp with. Look for somebody that's going to be a man or woman of God.

I hope I've said something in this book of Philemon that's going to make you go read the rest. Make you go and study the rest of it this week. That's just a little nugget for what God is doing. On our way to glory, we have to learn how to enjoy the trip. Now I'm going to say this final word. **When you purchase stuff, purchase for future. Purchase for quality.** I don't get anything based on the fad that's in right now because all these fads come and go and come again. If you shop based on the fad you will never ever have enough. You can take a simple nice elegant black dress and keep it for 40 years if you know how to go home and hang your clothes up. Take care of your things. Buy clothes that flatter your shape. You can't wear something that Beyoncé can wear. I can't wear what Beyoncé wear. I probably could but I'd keep it in the bedroom, because some of that stuff she wear I wouldn't go outside with. Just because you saw somebody with it on TV and they a size 2, don't mean it was meant for you.

In the same token, **pick people in your lives that are going to last for a long time.** Stop picking these short term people who you know on the first week they ain't going to make it. Pick people in your life that are long term. Look for qualities that you have but as well, other things that strengthen you. Bishop is my balancer, we're flopping roles now. It used to be that Bishop just was like, "Oh well whatever, let them bump their head you know." And I be like, "No they not finna bump they head, you ain't finna bump your head, you better get yourself together." Now Bishop is like, "Get yourself together or get out." And I'm like, "They are going to be alright, just let them bump they head." We're switching roles because his strength is my strength, and my strength is his strength. And so there are no weaknesses. Don't pick people that are weak in the same area that you're weak in so they can't talk about you. So then the leader becomes the follower. Pick people that are going to be long term, like you pick your garments that fit you well, that compliment you and that last forever.

Who's in your 5?

People I call friends, I've had for 20-25 even 30 years, and we push each other to the next level. I don't have any friends that aren't doing anything, because I don't sit on the seat of nothingness. And nothing from nothing leaves nothing. **Look at your 5 favorite people on your phone and determine their income level and you know what your income level is going to be**. If your favorite 5 is broke, you talking to them too much. Go talk to some of them other people down in your phone that got some money, and a job, and a career and a mindset to go somewhere. Change your 5! Who's your favorite 5? Are they gossipers? Who's your favorite 5? Who'd you talk to all day yesterday? Was it somebody that could encourage you and promote you and push you? Cause the person that did that needs to be your number one person to talk to all the time. The person that didn't do that, you need to cut them off because that was a waste of your time.

Closing Prayer

Lord we thank you for this early revelation and we thank you that in you we live and move and have our being. And we thank you that there is none like you in heaven or in earth. God we praise you for the information, we praise you for the information. We praise you for the information of grace and peace, the shalom of the Lord. What it should mean to us. What it should be in our lives. We thank you for the information, we thank you lord, we thank you lord, we thank you lord, we thank you lord. There is none like you, there is none like you, there is none like you. We bless your name God, we bless your name God, we bless your mighty name oh God. We bless your mighty name oh God. We bless your mighty name oh God. We bless your mighty name oh God.

CHAPTER 14

YOUR CALLING

BREAK EVERY CHAIN

Am I on Assignment?

God has given each of you a talent and you have a special gift that has been given to you to help the ministry and the pastor succeed. So when the church fails or falls it's because people have not used their given opportunity to make their gifts cause the church to be a better place. You cannot be content in just sitting in the pew. **You have to always ask God to give you another assignment.** Another ministerial assignment. Another work to do.

You have to have a work to do for God! And you have to have that assignment on your heart at all times. So whatever your assignment is you work diligently to fulfill and complete that assignment. And many of you are going to be given in your life many gifts and talents to be used to elevate the body of Christ in purpose and in assignment. And you have to pass the assignment test. What am I assigned to do? Am I doing that? No one should ever have to tell you what to do, because that's your assignment. That's your calling. You should be in place for your calling and be in place for your assignment. You are here to strengthen the body, you're here to make it better and make it right. To enhance and to develop those things that God has already assigned you to do.

And so we have to look at ministry like a construction phase. When we're building that building and the foundation goes up, it's dubbed. The foundation and the footing is done. A lot of people never understand that there's concrete down there that holds up these walls. **The higher you go the deeper you must dig to balance.** And in your spirit and in your hearts, the higher you're going to go the deeper you must dig to balance. So you must always be digging into the wells of God on how to perfect the area in which you have been assigned to do. You've been called to do. I'm not just talking about your gifts and your talents. I'm talking about what is it that God has called you to do.

207

Ring ring….God is calling YOU

As you sit in the pews, you must ask God, **"What is it that I am called to do?"** A calling is then my assignment. What is it that I'm assigned to do? What is it that I'm destined to do? What is it that I have purposed to do? And you must work on that assignment. If your assignment is the music ministry, then you must ask yourself, "Who am I seeking to come and be a part of the music ministry and the music team? What am I assigned to do? What hours am I laying aside to come over to the church and practice and get other musicians to come in and practice with me? What songs am I learning differently?" When you're on the praise team you learn your assignment. You say, "Okay I have these 8 songs I need to know. I need to perfect them because if that leader is out I need to be able to lead. If that leader is out I need to be able to lead." **There should be no hole in the ministry in which I have an assignment in.**

If I'm a preacher, I'm always ready to preach. I've learned I need to always be prepared. I need to always have a word from the Lord. I need to always have a sermon in my heart. Why? Because I been with God and I understand my assignment, I understand it's my destiny. **And so anything that I'm destined to do and assigned to do I've always wanted to do with excellence.** If I will cook you a meal, boy I will cook you a good one. I will cook you the kind that will have you sucking your fingers asking me, "What did you do to that pork chop? What did you do to that turkey wing?" I'm not just going to throw something together, because that means I wasn't assigned for it.

Keep your assignment in your heart…at all times

My assignment, the areas that I'm assigned in, should be blessed when I'm in them. When I'm in them I can see them flourishing because I have been assigned and I'm doing it well.

Assignment is more than just sitting down. Assignment stretches you. When I'm assigned whatever department I'm in gets better because I enhance it, I add to it. I'm better because of it. I'm looking for outfits that the praise team can wear all at once. I'm looking for clothing, I'm looking for things that we can do as a body of Christ. I'm looking for events. I'm looking for opportunities. I'm looking for stuff that couples in the church can do so I can bring it to the table. I don't get an assignment and then act like I don't have it because I don't want to complete it. No. **If I'm assigned to do it I'm, I'm destined to do it and I'm going to do it right.**

What hole can I fill?

Ask yourself, "Okay I'm going to this church. I'm a member of this church. What hole am I going to fill? What vision does the Apostle have that's not coming to pass that I know I can take up an assignment and be able to do? That I'll think about. That I'll do it. She won't even have to remind me." **Some of us take on assignments and we never do it.** Or somebody has to constantly remind us of the assignment that we say we have. You aren't called to that then. That's why some of us are shuffled around. Because if the area that you're in shows no growth, I don't see you getting better in, I don't see you coming forth in that area, then I need to move you cause that isn't your calling. That's not your assignment. And I venture to say you aren't even anointed to do it. Because when you finally get to the place where you're anointed, then there are no issues, there is no drama, you love to do it, you don't have to be reminded. You're focused on it. It's a blessing, it's a breakthrough. Cause I'm assigned to it. I'm called to it. And that's more than just your title. That's what you really do. Cause a lot of people have titles and they don't really do them.

The Assignment. The Calling. The Destiny.

They're called a Deacon but they don't check on the members. They're called the usher but they're mean. They're called to be the door keeper but they're always late. They say they're on the pastor advancement club but every time it comes time to do something for the pastor they murmur and complain. The assignment, the calling, the purpose in which God called you to do. **When you finally get in it, when you finally stand, when you finally work, when you finally do those things that cause increase because you were doing it. Now you've reached your calling.** And I love it so much I call other people about it now they want to do it. And now it's an increase. It's an interest. The calling, the assignment, the destiny. Write those 3 words down. The calling, the assignment, the destiny.

I want you to answer those 3 questions this week. What's my calling? What's my assignment? What's my destiny? Am I doing what I'm called to do? What I'm assigned to do? **Am I colliding with my destiny or do I just have a title but I'm really not doing anything?** Every day of your life when you wake it'll be on your mind. By the end of that day when I haven't done what I'm assigned to do I'm miserable. You can't be comfortable when you're not doing your assignment. You cannot be comfortable when you're not fulfilling your destiny. You can't be comfortable. And if you're comfortable you haven't found your calling yet. Cause if you can go to bed, "Oh well I'm an evangelist but I haven't talked to anybody about being saved today." If you can just go to bed and its okay, that's not your calling.

We must recognize that God is entrusting us, because that is what an assignment is, and our leader is entrusting us with a task. If we don't learn how to do what we are assigned to do, we will never be promoted. I don't know about you, but I have to go somewhere in God. I can't sit in kindergarten all my life waiting on another somebody to do what it is that I was assigned to do but didn't get done. You don't understand your anointing and you don't understand your assignment. So you act as though you're a private instead of a major. In fact, you act as if you're not even enlisted. There should not still be times in your life when your leader has to step in and get the ball rolling because you don't have enough energy to even give it a push. I'm on assignment, how about you? So the incompetence in your life shows up because when the light comes darkness is made known. Real leaders lead, everybody else follows. So what you say then is that you're not a leader, even amongst your peers. A real leader is going to rise to the top every time. It's like grease mixed in water, it's going to rise to the top.

Embrace your assignment. You're holding up somebody's salvation. You're holding up somebody else's plan, until you embrace your assignment. You're holding up somebody else's destiny. Hell is real and some of us will miss Heaven because of disobedience, because we're not on assignment. Some of us are going to miss heaven, just clean miss it, because you think you're doing wonderful and God says no. You're not even doing the assignment of your leaders much less your bible. You're not growing up, you're not pushing yourself, you're not getting in there studying. You mean God said to you to be a video producer and you won't even go on YouTube and see how to produce a video! Everything is an excuse with you. Everything has to be hand given to you. Even an eagle at some point kicks the baby birds out of the nest. And you either fly or die. God wants 100 %, because 99 ½ just won't do.

About The Author

Dr. Rice is the founding pastor of the Greater Harvest Christian Center Churches Worldwide (Inc.), which was founded in the year 1992. After Dr. Rice served in the evangelism field for eight years and as a local minister for four years, she was consecrated in the year 2004 as an Apostle in the city of Columbia, South Carolina where she served most of her junior and senior ministerial services. Chief Apostle Rice is the consecrated, elected, and appointed (2009–2015) Chief Apostle to the InterGlobal Association of Christian Churches Worldwide and works daily to insure global unity and pastoral networking to the fivefold ministry and to the body of Christ. Chief Apostle also serves as CEO of Rice Ministries International. This dynamic woman of the Cross is a noted soloist, psalmist and sought after revivalist with the gift of taking the body of Christ through exhortation and worship directly into the throne room of God.

She is the wife of Archbishop James Rice, whom she loves, respects, adores, and knows God sent him to her. She is the biological mother of three gifted, talented, and dedicated-to-God's-Kingdom Kids and the spiritual, Godmother, Mentor, Pastor, Coach, and Apostle to the nations. Bishop and Chief Apostle now grandparents of eight, were both born in Columbia, South Carolina, and now live in South Florida. They pastor Greater Harvest Christian Center Churches Worldwide South also known as GHCC South Florida.

Dr. J. G. Rice is a gift to the world, and to the Body of Christ, she is and has been a successful radio host, television personality, and professional instructor. She is a Chancellor of Harvest University International Bible College and President of West Harvest High School. She has numerous awards, certificates, and honors. Chief Apostle Rice is also a recording artist, and author of over 15 books including "It's All About the Kingdom" and her newly released books "Prayers From the Altar" and "The Transformation Factor." She is both a Teacher, Infuser, Orator, and a powerful Preacher. Dr. Rice is the founder of over 37 ministries, including Greater Harvest Christian Center Churches Worldwide and is Chief Apostle for many InterGobal Churches. As one educated, she believes in education and promotes actively against violence in her Circle 59' Ministry.

She is a life-changing conference speaker, revivalist, workshop host, and an all-round mentor, coach, and covering to the body of Christ. Apostle believes in Kingdom Living and Kingdom Protocol, and these two things operating in your life will bring a Kingdom blessing that will manifest here on earth. This is a true voice that must be heard in every nation, every city, every town, every house; every ear must hear what the Spirit has to say, through this teaching, preaching, prophetic, Apostolic gift to the church.

Her scripture for life is. "I'm just the voice of one crying in the wilderness, preparing the way of the Lord.—Chief Apostle Dr. J. G. Rice

DISCLAIMER-

THIS BOOK CONTAINS THE UNEDITED TESTMONIALS OF CURRENT OR PAST MEMBERS OF GREATER HARVEST CHRISTIAN CENTER CHURCHES WORLDWIDE-IGACCW. ALL WRITINGS ARE COMPOSED FROM THE WRITER'S PERSPECTIVE AND PERSONAL EXPERIENCE AND IS REPRESENTED AS THE TRUE AND ACCURATE FACTS AS THEY RECALL THEM. "THE TRANSFORMATION FACTOR" CONTRIBUTORS, IT'S AUTHOR- CHIEF APOSTLE DR. J. G. RICE, PUBLISHERS, NOR PUBLISHING COMPANY IS NOT HELD LIABLE FOR ANY INACCURACIES OR DISCREPANCIES AS TO THE TRUE OR REPRESENTED FACTS FROM OTHER INDIVIDUALS. THEIR TESTIMONY WAS CONTRIBUTED TO ENHANCE THEIR SPIRITUAL GROWTH AND AS A CAMPAIGN TO HELP OTHERS SUCCEED. THEY ARE NOT SEEKING NOR HAVE RECEIVED PAYMENT OR COMPENSATION FOR THEIR TESTIMONY AND WRITINGS.

www.ingramcontent.com/pod-product-compliance
Lightning Source LLC
La Vergne TN
LVHW051230080426
835513LV00016B/1512